MYTHICAL STAR SIGNS

BY
MARILYN REID

Published by Lulu.com
Copyright © 20th Nov. 2005 Marilyn Reid

Marilyn Reid
28 Glen Grove
Newtonmore
Scotland, U.K.

Phone: 01540 670036
Email: Marilyn@MarilynReid.com

ISBN 978-1-84753-623-5

Mythical Star Signs
This First Edition paperback first published in March 2007
by
Lulu.com

Email: Marilyn@MarilynReid.com

To my Son, Colin

The Sun, with all the planets revolving around it,
And depending on it,
Can still ripen a bunch of grapes
As though it had nothing else
In the Universe to do.

Galileo Galilei

Contents

Astrological Roots
Magic, Mystery, Michael Scot

From the dawn of history, people throughout the world have practiced magic to try to control human actions or natural events. In time, this belief and study of the natural and cosmic forces led to the development of religion, chemistry, medicine, astronomy and astrology, philosophy and science; not as separate subjects as we know them today, but as associated parts of a whole and developed system of belief.

This association was fundamental to the evolution of each of those parts and was the root system of the individual branches that sprung from them that we know and recognise today. For example, the great religions trusted today are linked, by a root, to Zoroastrianism, the first ever monotheist religion.

A universal religion, Zoroastrianism, in its earliest form, is based on one god of nature and the practice of good thoughts, good words, righteousness, and enlightenment through free will. (The Magi, true priests of Zorastrianism, known for practising magic, interpreting omens, dreams and astrological events, who followed the ancient doctrine, we know as the three wise men who followed the star of Bethlehem.) Zoroastrianism is thought to have been practised from the end of the stone age/beginning of the bronze age, until the present time.

By the early Middle Ages, nearly all Europeans believed in magic.

The clergy believed in its divine power, alchemists hoped to discover the philosopher's stone and sought the elixir of life, and students of medicine studied astrology for three years before they could become doctors.

Between the 12th and 13th centuries, a great sharing of knowledge shone like a beacon of light from East to West and North to South. The enlightened gathered at great centres of learning in the East and West such as Toledo in Europe. Alchemy and astrology became closely related because of the belief that each heavenly body represented and controlled a certain metal. It was thought that the sun represented gold; the moon silver; Mars iron; Venus copper; and Mercury, mercury or quick silver, and that the positions of these bodies influenced success or failure, sickness and health.

The work of the alchemists and their preparation and study of chemical substances, led to the development of the sciences of chemistry and medicine, and it wasn't until about the sixteenth century that astronomy began to be separated from astrology. This only happened once the Earth itself was accepted as one of the heavenly bodies.

Where previously priests were in charge of the divination of the royals and their nations, by the Middle Ages, it was the scholars, mathematicians and philosophers who were charting the correlations between celestial objects and human and earthly affairs. These astrologers were known as the Mathematici.

Outside the university walls, belief in the planetary powers was so wide spread that rulers retained their own personal court astrologers. Frederick the second (1194-1250), Emperor of Rome, employed a Scotsman as his, the incredible Michael Scot.

Known in his lifetime as "The Great Magician", Michael Scot's reputation as a translator, astronomer, mathematician, alchemist and astrologer, was spread throughout Europe and the East. Michael was born in 1175 at Balwearie, in Fife, Scotland.

At the time of Michael's birth, Geoffrey of Monmouth's "History of the King's of Britain", which included 'The Prophecies of Merlin', was a best seller. Geoffrey's work reflects the exploits of Rome and France in the twelfth century and echoes the careers of the emperors of Rome. By the time Michael Scot was a young man, the stories of Merlin, the wizard of the court of King Arthur, were very popular indeed, and so, with a strong belief in magic the bright, young Michael set out to educate himself. He studied at Oxford, Bologna, and Paris, before he became court astrologer to Frederick, the young Emperor of Rome. Legends of Michael's power as a magician grew around the world and served as a theme for many writers including Dante.

At home in Scotland, he was also a legend, and one story tells that Michael was already a powerful magician before he travelled to Europe, due to his encounter with a white serpent. In Scottish culture, a white serpent is supposed to give skill to physicians. The serpent was a sacred animal in Scotland and according to tradition, it slept all winter long until Beira, the winter goddess, was overthrown by Bride, the goddess of growth. A part of the body of the serpent had to be cooked and he who first tasted the juice of the serpent obtained the power to cure disease and might become a seer, it was believed.

One day, when Michael was young, he was travelling the hills near Laggan in Scotland with two friends, when they heard a loud hissing sound, and when they looked up the hill they saw with horror a great white serpent coming towards them at great speed. Michael's two friends ran off in fear but Michael stood waiting for it holding his staff up high. When it attacked him, he struck the serpent three times with such ferociousness that its body was cut in three parts.

He caught up with his friends and told them he had slain the serpent and they carried on with their journey. By night fall, they had reached the house of an old woman who invited them to stay the night. The friends told the kind woman about their adventure with the huge white serpent.

The wise old woman informed them that the white serpent was no ordinary serpent and that if the head part managed to crawl to a stream and bathe in it, it could then re-unite with its other parts and become whole again. If, however, a man could stop it reaching the stream, it would surely die. She advised Michael to go and find it again and take its middle part, or it would appear forever, again and again, to attack him until it killed him. Michael too her advice and set out again. Before long he returned with the middle part of the serpent's body. The old lady promptly popped it into a cauldron full of water that was hanging above a blazing fire.

Later, the old woman asked Michael to keep an eye on the pot while she slept, and once the serpent's body was cooked, he removed it from the fire. Lifting the lid, he dipped his finger into the juices of the serpent's body. The tip of his finger burned so he thrust it immediately into his mouth. Suddenly new light and knowledge broke in upon him, and he discovered that he had the power to foretell events, to work magic and to read the minds of people.

There are many myths surrounding Michael's powers, how he got them, what he did with them, but in truth, Michael applied himself with such diligence at Paris, he was known academically as Michael the Mathematician. He attained equal distinction in sacred letters and divinity, and had the degree of doctor of theology conferred upon him.

Later, he travelled, and at the celebrated college at Padua, Italy, Michael eminently distinguished himself by his essays on judicial astrology. From there, he travelled to Spain where at Toledo he translated from Arabic to Latin, Aristotle's nineteen books on the history of animals. This work brought him to the attention of Frederick the 2nd who invited him to his court to be his royal astrologer. Whilst there, Michael translated, at the Emperor's desire, the greater part of the works of Aristotle and wrote, at royal request, an original work entitled "Liber introductorius sive Indicia Quaestionum", for the use of young students. His other important works included one which was on the "Opinions of Astrologers". Michael worked at Frederick's court for several years and afterwards, when he resigned from his residency, he took up medicine and also acquired a great reputation for this.

Before he died, Michael returned to Britain and, after spending time at the court of Edward the first, he returned to Scotland. By the time he returned to Scotland, his reputation had gained him the name of Wizard, not least due to the writings of his contemporaries such as Dante and Boccaccie.

Michael's work as a translator of Greek texts from the Arabic was of great importance in western European intellectual history. His translation in Sicily, in 1217, of Al-Birruji's 'On the Sphere' literally revolutionised the study of astronomy, particularly the planets, and his work on alchemy and judicial astrology made him a legend at home and abroad.

Buried at Melrose Abbey under the western window, Michael's body lies in grand company, and even the death of Scotland's famous wizard brought about new stories, particularly one relating to Michael's body being buried with his famous book of magic. (Hundreds of years later, Sir Walter Scott wrote about this in the notes accompanying his 'The Lay of the Last Minstrel'.) However, Michael Scot's magic book is amongst the manuscript collections of the John Ryland's Library. A strange work, this has only added to the number of myths and mystery surrounding the name of this very learned and special man whose astrological roots grew in Scotland.

The Celestial Zodiac

Introduction to Western Signs

To early man, who read the stars avidly, the night sky precessions, and their regularity were the focus of wonder and awe. And, recognising resemblance in them of well known objects and living beings, he believed divine power had put them in the sky. He called the precessions "constellations", which are Latin for two words, "con" - together, and "stella" - the stars. The constellations were recorded as by the Babylonian priests of Mesopotamia as being formed of twelve celestial groups.

The Babylonian priest-astrologers, who knew only five planets as well as the moon and the sun, noticed that these seven heavenly bodies appeared together within one of the star constellations at exactly the same season of the year. They noticed too, that the sun seemed to rise every month in a different constellation, returning to rise again in the first, after visiting the twelfth. So, the Mesopotamians assumed the entire procession was rotating in a circular motion. This circle, in the ancient Greek tongue, became known, as it is today, as the Zodiac, combining the Greek "zoon" - animal, with "kyklos" - circle. A celestial circle of twelve, which was made up monthly of animals, and each, being divine, was the subject of myth and legend.

Around the 17th century B.C., Mesopotamian boundary stones

carried the astrological symbols, including the frightening scorpio-man from their mythology which is identified by some as Sagittarius.

Today the symbols of the Western Zodiac are well known by their Greek association, but they signify something far older than we know, way back to the time of the Mesopotamia, the ancient cradle of civilisation, who developed the idea of the Zodiac.

Since these ancient times, the position of the Earth has changed in space so the symbols no longer represent the time the sun was in the related star constellations exactly. Take, for example, the first constellation, Aries, (March 21st to April 20th). At the present time the sun is actually still in Pisces on March 23rd. However, most astrologers today still use the traditional dates.

The myths and legends associated with the Western Zodiac symbols are wonderful stories. The most ancient association comes from the twelve tablets of the oldest written story on Earth, The Epic of Gilgamesh, where the scorpion-people are mentioned, in tablet nine.

The King of Urak, Gilgamesh, set out on a quest for immortality to the Garden of the Sun, the land of everlasting life. The journey takes him to the mountain of the horizon, Mount Mashu, where the Sun's gate was. In order to reach the Garden, he would have to pass through the gate. The Sun set from the mountain of the horizon and emerged from it to rise. But the garden gate was guarded by two scorpion-people who guarded the Sun's path. Gilgamesh gains entrance to the next level, eventually accepting his mortality. The entire Epic, is thought to be 3 - 5 thousand years old.

The Greeks adopted the celestial Zodiac and immediately linked it to their own myths, and this book introduces some of the myths and legends about each symbol of the Western Zodiac from various cultures.

But other parts of the world have their own Zodiacs, and so following the signs of the Western Zodiac, in this book, you will be introduced to and discover the Egyptian Zodiac, the Chinese Zodiac, and the Australian Zodiac. We have only recently discovered, and are just beginning to understand, the astro-archeological evidence left behind for us by the ancients. I hope you will enjoy this introduction to some of it, and the legends behind the mythical star signs of the Zodiacs.

Symbol of the Golden Fleece - Aries!

Aries, first sign of the Zodiac, is a fire sign and astrologers believe it is ruled by the planet Mars.

(March 21 - April 20)

Mars, after the Romans came into contact with the Greeks, became the god of war in Roman mythology. To the ancient Romans, Mars was important because they believed him to be the father of Romulus and Remus, the legendary founders of Rome.

The Greek god of war was Ares, and the Romans gave Mars similar characteristics to that of Ares. Before going to war, the Romans offered sacrifices to the god Mars and they named the planet after him. The word 'martial' means 'war like', is based on the god's name.

The wolf and the woodpecker are associated with Mars and the month of March is named after him. Originally, Mars was a god of farmland and fertility. Since ancient times, the area enclosed by a bend in the River Tiber in Rome has been called the Field of Mars.

The star constellation of Aries was given its name of ram from the ancient Babylonians, (the Latin for ram is Aries), because of its important significance in their society. The ram was one of the first animals early man worshipped even in prehistoric times, and occupied an eminent place in the old days. The sun passes through the constellation of Aries at the time of the Spring equinox, and to the ancients this was significant of renewal and the beginning of life, hence Aries was chosen as the first sign.

The Greeks adopted the celestial and zodiacal ram from the ancients, and linked its existence with one of their own myths.

The legend tells how the ram was placed in the skies by Zeus himself. It was the most famous ram of all, the winged ram with the golden fleece. The ram had saved Phrixus and his sister Helle from the alter where they were to be offered as a sacrifice to Zeus.

The golden ram carried them on his back and flew through the air across the sea towards Colchis. On the way, Helle slipped from the ram's back and was drowned in the sea. The ram continued and carried Phrixus safely to Colchis, where Phrixus sacrificed the ram to Zeus, and then presented the golden fleece to his father-in-law, the King of Colchis. The fleece was fastened to an oak tree and guarded by a dragon night and day until Jason and the Argonauts retrieved it.

Zeus was so moved by the ram's fate, that he honoured it by placing it in the heavens. The place where Helle met her watery fate was named after her and remains to this day to be known by Hellespoint or Dordanelles, a narrow strait in North West Turkey.

The star constellation Aries is in the northern sky and its brightest star is Hamel. It is a spring sign of the Zodiac and it lies between Pisces and Taurus. The sun enters Aries at the Spring equinox about the 20th of March.

Zeus in Disguise – Taurus!

Taurus, second sign of the Zodiac, is an earth sign and astrologers believe it is ruled by the planet Venus.

(April 21 - May 21).

According to Roman mythology, Venus was born fully grown from the foam of the Mediterranean Sea and came to land on the island of Cyprus. She married Vulcan, a lame and ugly blacksmith, but then she had an affair with Mars, the Roman god of war. She also fell in love with Adonis, a mortal.

Originally, Venus was a protector of gardens, and she became a major goddess to the Romans. A goddess of love, to both the Romans and the Greeks, (she was Aphrodite to the Greeks), she symbolised the creative force that sustains all life. One of her sons was Cupid, the Roman god of love, and the other Aeneas, was a Trojan ancestor of the legendary founders of Rome. The Romans believed that the family of Julius Caesar was descended from Venus, through Aeneas.

A famous myth, The Judgement of Paris, tells that there was once a prize of a golden apple reserved for the most beautiful goddess. Venus, Juno and Minerva all claimed the prize. The god Jupiter ordered Paris,

who was the son of King Priam of Troy, to choose. Paris chose Venus.
In revenge, Minerva and Juno made sure that Troy was destroyed during
the Trojan war.

The early astrologers, founders of astronomy, called the most
brilliant group of stars by the Latin name Taurus (bull), because of the
bull's important position in nature for them and their myths, for he was
to them a symbol of procreation, just as he had been to prehistoric man
as we know from his earliest cave paintings.

The bull was worshipped throughout the East and the Egyptians
had a sacred bull. The bull-fight of today, has its roots in a powerful
ancient fertility rite of the ancients from Spain and Latin America.

In Greek tradition, some of the stars in the constellation of Taurus
were originally a group of sisters, the Hyades, who were known as the
Nymphs of Nysa because they lived on Mount Nysa. The god of all gods
to them, Zeus, had a particular affection for them because they had
nursed his son, Dionysus.

One day, their brother went out hunting and he was killed by a lion.
The sisters were so heartbroken with grief, they committed suicide. Zeus
responded by changing them into a star cluster and placing them in the
constellation, Taurus the Bull. One of them, Aldebaran, shines brightly
and represents the bull's eye, and the others, in a V-shape, form the
horns and the nose of the bull. Because the Hyades appear in the sky
during rainy seasons, the Greeks believed them to be messengers of
Spring showers and Autumn storms. Their name means "to rain" in
Greek.

Zeus eventually joined them. He fell in love with the beautiful
daughter of the Phoenician King. Her name was Europa and he
abducted her by assuming the shape and colour of a snow-white, golden
horned bull. He carried her on his back while he swam all the way from
her country to Crete. This romantic journey gave Europe its name, and
Zeus remains in the heavens in his bovine disguise.

Venus is the brightest of all the sparkles in the sky because her orbit
lies inside the Earth's so she can never be further than 47 degrees from
the Sun, this we know today.

Silver jewel of the night sky, just as lovely as ever, Venus and her history continue to inspire the creative processes of painters, poets, and our imaginations!

The Guiding Lights – Gemini!

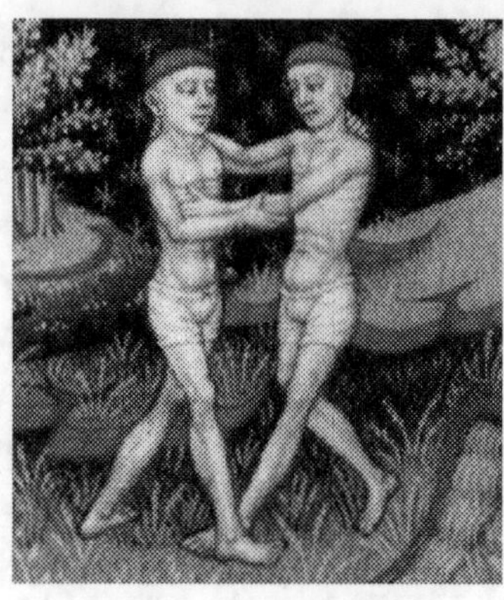

Gemini, third sign of the Zodiac, is an air sign and astrologers believe it is ruled by the planet Mercury.

(May 22 - June 21)

According to Roman Mythology, Mercury was the messenger of the gods who was the offspring of the god Jupiter and Maia. Maia, his mother, was one of the seven sisters, the Pleiadas, daughters of the Titan, Atlas.

Mercury delivered his messages with miraculous speed because he wore winged sandals. He also wore a broad brimmed winged hat and carried a winged staff which had two snakes curled around it and he was worshipped by the Romans as the god of commerce, property and wealth. The words merchant, commerce and merchandise are related to his name. The Romans also considered Mercury crafty and deceptive and he was also the god of games and storytelling.

Because Mercury resembled the messenger of the Greeks, Hermes, the Romans associated him with many of the Greek myths of Hermes.

The word 'Gemini' in Latin, means twins and Greek legend regards the stars of the constellation of Gemini as a symbol of loyalty and deep affection because of their association with Castor and Pollux.

Castor and Pollux were twin brothers who were so attached to each other that they not only lived together, but wanted to die together. They were born to Leda after her seduction by Zeus. Castor was mortal, Pollux was immortal.

When Castor was slain in battle, Pollux was so overcome with grief that he pleaded with the great Zeus to either revive his twin brother or to make him share the same fate. This expression of brotherly love touched Zeus, but he could not grant the request, instead he allowed Pollux to divide his days so that he could spend one day with the gods in Olympus, and the next in the world below the Earth, Hades, the world of the mortals. (In Greek mythology, Hermes the messenger, ruled the underworld Hades)

One tradition states that it was because of this shining example of true brotherly love that the star constellation of Gemini the twins came into being. To acknowledge the twins' mutual devotion, Zeus placed them together in the sky, now as the heavenly twins.

The honours bestowed on Castor and Pollux did not end there, for Poseidon, the god of the seas, rewarded them for their devotion by putting them in control of the waves and winds. And, aware of their power, sailors throughout history duly made them their patrons. Before the invention of the compass, the bright twin stars helped sailors in navigation.

Gemini is a northern constellation and it lies between Taurus and Cancer. Castor is a double star and Pollux is a bright orange star, the nearest giant star to Earth.

The planet Mercury is the nearest major planet to the Sun. Interestingly, when in Mercury's sky, the Sun sometimes loops backwards. If this happens at sunrise, Mercury has a double dawn! The Sun enters Gemini on May 21st.

Mercury was used to denote the chemical element of atomic 80, also called 'quicksilver'. A heavy silvery white metal that liquidates at room temperature, its rapid motion is held to be characteristic of the Winged

Messenger, Mercury.

Castor and Pollux, those shining guiding lights, have caught people's attention since the early days and they were honoured again in more recent times by America when the first space craft ever to carry two men into orbit towards the stars was named, Gemini!

Star-Sign of Bravery - Cancer!

Cancer, fourth sign of the Zodiac, is a water sign, and astrologers believe it is ruled by the moon.

(June 22 - July 22)

Through the centuries people have gazed at the moon, worshipped it and studied it, and since ancient times, people have measured time by the phases of the moon.

Christians observe Easter on a date that varies every year because it is related to the full moon. People in Muslim countries still use a calendar with 354 days, or 12 synodic lunar months.

Early people around the Earth believed the moon was a god or goddess. The ancient Romans had two moon goddesses, Luna and Diana. Diana was the goddess of the hunt too. Her bow was a moon crescent and her arrows were moonbeams.

Both the Greeks and the Romans believed in a goddess who had three faces, Hecate. As Hecate herself, she was the moon in its dark form, as Diana she was the waxing moon, and as Luna, she was the full moon.

The Aborigines of Australia regarded the moon as male, because of its association with the female menstrual cycle. The moon was linked with fertility and was accorded great magical status. A solar eclipse was interpreted as the Moon-man uniting with the Sun-woman.

The word 'Cancer' is Latin for the Greek "grapsias" meaning 'crab', and the choice of the crab to symbolise the constellation goes far back in time to the Chaldean star-gazers.

The star constellation of Cancer formed the background for the sun when the sun reached the summer solstice. This is the moment when the sun, having reached its most northerly position, reverses, and begins its journey southward. It was this returning movement that gave birth to the name 'crab' for this lovely constellation, not its likeness to the animal. The summer solstice can be June 20th, 21st or 22nd.

The Egyptians represented this sign with the figure of a scarab. According to their mythology this beetle possessed the power of the perpetual renewal of life. It became their symbol of eternity. The ancient Egyptians would present people of distinction with a special scarab medal to honour them. To ensure resurrection, the Egyptian dead were entombed with a valuable scarab ornament.

In Greek mythology, the Crab was placed in the sky by the goddess Hera, who raised it to eternal life in the skies as a reward for its bravery. The hero Hercules, on one of his twelve labours, had to kill the many-headed dragon named Hydra. As soon as he cut one of her heads off, two new heads would immediately take their place making the task almost impossible. The goddess Hera, who was the Greek goddess of life, was hostile towards Hercules because he was the son of Zeus and one of his mistresses. Hera had been both a wife and a sister to Zeus. Hera, concerned for the dragon Hydra, sent a crab to nip Hercules' foot while he was fighting the dragon. But Hercules crushed it to death, so Hera gave it eternal light and placed it in the skies.

The early astrologers included the moon in their list of planets as well as the sun, hence the belief that the moon is the ruling 'planet' of Cancer.

To the Babylonians, the moon was known as Sin or Nanner, the most powerful of sky gods. Some American Indian tribes believed the moon and the sun were brother and sister.

Today, some people still worship the moon and some plant their seeds in its pale beams of light. A symbol of the peaceful exploration of space, and vital to our very existence, no nation owns the moon. In 1967 more than ninety nations signed a space treaty that declares neither the moon nor any other natural body in space may be claimed by any country or used for military purposes.

The star constellation Cancer is a northern constellation and it lies between Gemini and Leo. It contains an open star cluster named Praesepe. Open star clusters contain a few dozen to a few hundred stars and are young. The Sun enters Cancer about June 21st.

Crowned in Stars - Leo!

Leo, fifth sign of the Zodiac, is a fire sign and astrologers believe it is ruled by the Sun.

(July 23 - August 22)

In the ancient days, Sun worship was a religious practice that developed as people came to associate the Sun with the growing season and with warmth. The Sun was sacred to the Aztec, Inca and Maya peoples who live in Central and South America, and some kings, queen's and emperors, believed themselves to be brothers, sisters, or even children, of the Sun. These people came to be worshipped as gods.

For hundreds of years, the Japanese worshipped their emperor as a descendant of the Sun goddess, Amaterusu-O-Mi-Kami. Ameterusu is both the Sun goddess who ruled all the gods, and the mother-goddess who ensures fertility. She is the principal deity in the Shinto religion of Japan and emperors were said to be descendant from her.

Once, when she shut herself in her cave, the whole world became darkened and no plants could grow. The other gods played music and offered her presents to make her return.

Shinto, which means "the way of the spirits", was so named in the 8th century to distinguish it from Buddhism, from which it incorporated many features. It emerged from the nature worship of Japanese folk religions. In 1945, Shintoism lost its official status, but in 1995, there were still nearly 3 million Shintoists. This worship continues today.

To the Inca people, the Inca emperor is also a direct descendant of a Sun god. The Sun God, Inti. In the 11th century they established their capital, Cuzco, the Sacred City of the Sun, where they built huge temples and fortresses which they covered in sheets of gold. Today, every year on the 24th of June, Cuzco celebrates the festival of Inti Raymi. This festival was the most important festival of the Inca empire whose religion was based on the cult of the Sun.

Over 200,000 people come together at the complex of Sacsayhauman, Sacred House of the Sun, to witness the beautiful spectacle of the year where more than 500 actors proudly bring their past to life. Everyone, including tourists, gets involved to enjoy the Inca's special day.

The word Leo, is Latin for 'lion'. The star constellation of Leo lies between Cancer and Virgo. Easy to recognise, the lion's head looks like a sickle. Its brightest star is Regulus.

The majestic figure of the Lion has always produced feelings of awe amongst people, and early opinion states that the constellation was given its name in association with the fiery ferocity characteristic of the Lion. However, Greek mythology tells a different story. According to the Greeks, Zeus placed the lion amongst the stars in honour of the outcome of Hercules first labour.

In the first of Hercules' twelve labours, Hercules had to kill the Nemean Lion. The lion, borne by Selene the moon goddess, was dropped to Earth on Mount Tretus, near Nemea, by Selene, as a punishment for an unfulfilled sacrifice. Selene set the lion to prey upon her own people. All attempts to kill it had been unsuccessful, as this mystical creature was invulnerable to stone, iron and bronze.

After meeting a peasant whose son had fallen victim to the lion, Hercules determined to slay it. Attacking it with arrows, his club and his sword, Hercules found none of those could harm it. When he found out that the lion's den had two entrances, he blocked one of them and when the Nemean Lion came out, he strangled it with his bare hands. He carried its body to the mourning father and together they brought an offering to Zeus.

Leo was placed in the sky to dwell forever, his head crowned with a beautiful sickle of stars. A northern constellation, Leo lies between Cancer and Virgo. Easy to recognise, its brightest star is Regulus.

North of Leo is the little lion, Leo Minor, which is hard to see. The Sun enters Leo about July 23rd.

Symbol of Woman - Virgo!

Virgo, sixth sign of the Zodiac is an earth sign, and astrologers believe it is ruled by the planet Mercury.

(August 23 - September 22)

Tradition states that Mercury was the messenger of the gods and in Roman mythology Mercury was the god of roads and travel. He could deliver his messages with great speed because he wore winged sandals called talaria. Mercury also wore a broad brimmed hat and carried a winged staff.

In those ancient days, most messengers wore a hat similar to Mercury's to protect them from the sun as they travelled on long journeys delivering their messages. They also carried a staff, to identify themselves so they could travel freely. Mercury's staff or caduceus, had two snakes curled around it. Later, Virgo's ruling planet became associated with magic and science.

The word "Virgo", in Latin, means "virgin" and world wide respect for woman in the ancient days ensured her position in one of the twelve houses of the Zodiac.

Almost every culture in the world worshipped both the virginity and the fruitfulness of woman who, in their eyes, ensured the continuance of the world. To many, the constellation of Virgo was named after their divine goddesses who, in time, were placed in the sky for protection.

One of them, Astrea, was of major importance to the ancients. She had experienced the golden ages of the world's young days, and, although she was a goddess, she lived on Earth. She symbolised innocence and justice, but when sin raised its head and purity began to disappear, there seemed no place on Earth for this divine, virtuous beauty. To keep her from corruption, and ultimate destruction, the gods raised her from the moral mire and placed her in the pure skies.

The fathers of astronomy and astrology, the Babylonians, chose Ishtar, the mother of all life and the goddess of love, as their divine female symbol. She survives in the Hebrew bible as Esther, the queen of Persia and saviour of her people.

In Peru, the Incas identified the constellation of Virgo with "the earth's mother". Originally, for the Arabs, the constellation was symbolised by an ear of corn, which later came to be called "the innocent maiden". Each culture who placed a woman in the skies, depicted her carrying a sheaf of corn in her arms, the symbol of fertility.

Virgo was the constellation through which the sun passed at the very season when the harvest was ripening. In classical times, this "house" of the Zodiac was known as "Ceres". Ceres was the protector of corn and the goddess of grain from whose name comes the word "cereal".

The Greek's story of how the virgin came to occupy her place in the heavens, tells of Icarius. Icarius was being instructed by Dionysus in the art of growing grapes and making wine. Icarius became an expert and shared his wine with many of his friends. Never having experienced intoxication, they imagined Icarius had tried to poison them and they killed him. Later, they buried his body under a pine tree.

When Icarius did not return home, his daughter Erigone, took his dog and went to look for him. discovering his body in its shallow grave, Erigone was so distraught by grief she took her own life by hanging herself from that very same pine tree. The gods placed the virgin in the skies to become the constellation Virgo.

The constellation Virgo contains and abundance of faint galaxies, as well as the first quasar to be recognised. This quasar, (a star like object emitting powerful radio waves), is known as 3C 273. Virgo also houses one of the largest galaxies in the known universe, M87. Its brightest star is Spica. Virgo lies on the celestial equator between Leo and Libra.

The Sun enters Virgo about the 23rd of August.

Harmony and Balance - Libra!

Libra, seventh sign of the Zodiac, is an air sign and astrologers believe it is ruled by the planet Venus.

(September 23 - October 22)

Venus is the only planet named after a goddess. The Romans named the planet after their goddess of love and beauty who was born full grown from the foam of the Mediterranean Sea, and came to land on the island of Cyprus.

To the Aztecs, Venus was one of the symbols of the god Tiahuizcalpantecuhtli, as was the feathered serpent, Quetzalcoatl. The Aztecs believed their god ruled the sky at noon, the twelfth hour of the day, and rituals were performed when the planet Venus was aligned with the Pleiades. The Pleiades, sometimes called the seven sisters, were known to the Aztecs as Tianquiztli. The temple of the god Tlahuizcalpantecuhtli is at Tula, Mexico.

The ancient Mayans used the windows and doorways of their buildings as astronomical sightings for the planet Venus. At Uxmal, the buildings are aligned in the same direction. The Mayans knew the motions of Venus with amazing accuracy for she was Kukulcan to them, the planet of warfare.

Many offerings were made to Venus and the Sun. Apparently, some people would stop up their chimneys so that no light from Venus could enter their houses and cause harm.

The old astrologers gave this constellation of stars its name of Libra, the Latin word for "balance". The constellation first appeared in the Julian calendar in 46B.C. at which time a comet appeared during the same year as Caesar's assassination and it states that the comet took Caesar's soul to heaven. It is believed the same comet appeared in 531, 1106, and 1680; its next appearance is expected in 2255.

Libra is the age old symbol of justice, harmony and balance, and can be found between Scorpius and Virgo. To the Italians, French, Germans, Anglo-Saxons, and Romans, the constellation was the scales, yet the Greeks did not recognise Libra as the scales but included it as the claws of the Scorpion. The Arabs followed the Greeks and included it as part of the scorpion's claws.

However, previously, the Egyptians, Hebrews, Persians and Syrians, all called the constellation the "weigh beam" or "scale beam".

One of the volcanoes on the planet Venus is called Sif, after the Norse goddess. Sif was the wife of Thor, the almighty god of thunder. Sif was a very loyal wife and considered to be a symbol of fidelity. The malicious god Loki, once cut her long blond tresses and when Thor found out, he lost control of his anger and grabbed Loki threatening to break his nose.

Loki cried out for mercy and promised Thor that he would convince the dwarfs to craft very refined hair of pure gold, which would grow like natural hair from Sif's head, which he did.

The scales are thought to symbolise the weighing of man's soul, determining his innocence or guilt and even his destiny.

The Sun enters Libra at the northern autumnal equinox, about the 23rd September, when day and night are almost equally balanced, just like the universe.

The Scorpion with the Heart of Antares - Scorpio!

Scorpio, eighth sign of the Zodiac, is a water sign and astrologers believe it is ruled by the planet Mars.

(23 October – 21 November)

To the Romans, Mars was the god of war and, after Jupiter, was the most important god. The month of March is named after him. His Greek equivalent is Ares. One legend relates to Ares' love for Venus and the trap made for them by her husband Vulcan, and from early times this became a favourite subject for artists.

The wolf and the woodpecker were regarded as sacred to Mars. In astrological belief the influence of the planet Mars is associated with combative, aggressive, or masculine qualities.

In Hindu mythology, the planet Mars is known as Mangala. The planet is identified with the war god Karttikeya. Karttikeya was born from six eyes of the god Sira into a lake near Madras. From the sparks, six children were created who were nursed by the Pleiades, (also known as the seven sister stars). But once, Parvati, who was Sira's wife, embraced them so tightly, that they became one body with six heads. This new-born became the war god Karttikeya who is often depicted as having six heads with twelve arms riding a peacock.

Scorpio the Scorpion, is the symbol of the constellation Scorpius. (Scorpius is the Latin for Scorpion) More than any other star constellation, Scorpius resembles its given name. If you live in the northern hemisphere of the Earth, you will see Scorpius crawl across the southern sky, close to the horizon. But in the southern hemisphere, it passes high in the sky. With its striking tail, it is easy to recognise. The scorpion has survived on the Earth for over 400 million years and was revered by the ancients who preserved its image in stone.

In traditional belief, the flesh of the scorpion was thought to be a cure for its own sting. Ancient writers also said that when surrounded by fire, a scorpion will commit suicide by stinging itself.

The celestial Scorpion once had claws but Julius Caesar cut them off to form the constellation Libra. But wherever you are, you can always recognise Scorpius by its bright heart, lit by the brilliant red supergiant star, Antares. Antares is so bright, it is often mistaken for the red planet Mars when they are close together. Antares is three hundred times as big as the Sun and three thousand times the Sun's luminosity. Scorpius surely has a strong, brave heart!

To the ancient Greeks, the constellation Scorpius was related to the death of the hunter Orion. One story tells how Orion fled the Scorpion by swimming the sea to the island of Delos to see his lover Athena. Apollo, seeking to punish Athena, joined her and challenged her hunting skills by daring her to shoot a black dot approaching the island from the water. Athena met the challenge and unknowingly killed her lover.

Another story states that Artemis, the great huntress and goddess, wished to acknowledge the Scorpion's deed of killing Orion by its sting, for it had done so at her bidding after Orion had boasted that he was superior to even the fiercest animal in stamina, strength, and speed. Artemis placed the celestial Scorpion in the gallery of stars.

Other sources say Gaia, the Earth goddess, placed the Scorpion's image in the night sky because she was displeased at Orion's wanting to kill all the Earth's wild animals. So she sent a giant scorpion to attack Orion.

There are many variations of the story of Orion and the Scorpion.

In the sky today, it looks as if the scorpion is still chasing Orion, since Artemis also placed Orion in the sky as a constellation.

The Orion constellation is the most conspicuous of all constellations. Equatorial, it is visible in both hemispheres and its brilliance shines out from the bright red star Betelgeuse, which marks Orion's left shoulder, and the blue-white star Rigel, marks his right foot.

The Great Nebula lies in the middle of his sword. This is the nearest and brightest nebula visible to the naked eye and it is busy making new stars. It can be seen with binoculars. The famous Horsehead nebula in Orion's belt is difficult to see but you will find fantastically beautiful photographs of it on NASA's web site in the public gallery.

Scorpius, in the southern sky, is a rich part of the Milky Way, with good clusters of stars. One of these, Scorpius X-1, is the first X-ray source outside our Solar system. Scorpius lies between Libra and Sagittarius.

The Sun enters Scorpius about the 23rd October.

Unselfish Heart of a Million Stars - Sagittarius!

Sagittarius, ninth sign of the Zodiac, is a fire sign and astrologers believe it is ruled by the planet Jupiter.

(22 November – 20 December)

According to Roman mythology, Jupiter was the king of gods and ruler of the Universe. He was originally a god of the sky, thunder and lightning, and he had the power to control the Earth's weather, fine and fair, wild, windy and stormy. Jupiter made certain that mortals lived out their lives according to their fate.

A son of Saturn, Jupiter and the other children of Saturn overthrew him, and Jupiter took his place. Jupiter's brothers were the gods Neptune and Pluto. His sisters were Ceres, Juno and Vesta. Jupiter was also the father of the nine Muses who inspired art, poetry and learning.

The Romans built a wonderful temple for Jupiter on the Capitoline hill, where they had shrines to Jupiter, Juno and Minerva. The goddess Minerva was said to have sprung from Jupiter's head. Jupiter's symbols were the oak tree, eagle and thunderbolt.

Jupiter is the largest planet in our Solar system and is the second brightest after Venus. A giant, it would take 1,000 Earths to fill its volume! Jupiter has 16 known moons. The largest four, although individually named, are known collectively as Gililean Satellites since they were first discovered by Galileo the Italian astronomer in 1610 with one of the earliest telescopes.

The symbol for Sagittarius, is the Archer and the word comes from the Latin sagitta, 'arrow' and sagittary, which means 'centaur', in particularly one very special centaur who was a great archer and from whom the star constellation Sagittarius is named.

Sagittarius, according to Greek mythology is Chiron, the Centaur. A centaur is a creature with the torso of a man and the body of a horse. Chiron (Sagittarius), was placed among the stars by the god of all gods, Zeus, as a result of his unselfishness. Chiron was the most famous of all centaurs, his skills were outstanding. He excelled in the arts of healing, teaching, prophesying and hunting.

He had no equal in performing acts of kindness. By accident, he was pierced with a poisoned arrow from the bow of Heracles in one of his legs. Heracles immediately removed the arrow from Chiron's leg but the wound never healed and caused Chiron great pain. So great was his pain, that he wished for death but, being immortal, even death could not relieve his suffering.

Meantime, a Titan named Prometheus, who was tethered to a rock in the dark, dismal abyss of Tartarus, which is far below Hades, appealed to Zeus to end his suffering. Zeus agreed to free Prometheus, only if someone would take his place. Chiron gladly volunteered to end the pain he was suffering. To reward him for this noble deed, Zeus elevated Chiron to the stars to form the constellation Sagittarius. Chiron taught humans to read the skies and the Argonauts were guided by his image in the sky.

To the early ancients, the Babylonians, Sagittarius was Enkidu, Gilgamesh's friend from the oldest epic in the world, the Epic of Gilgamesh. Later generations, in the time of the Bible, felt that the star constellation represented the bow God is said to have sent as the everlasting token of God's covenant with man, after he saved Noah from the great deluge.

A very large constellation, many objects reside in Sagittarius. The brightest star in the constellation is Alpha Centauri. It is the closest star to the Sun, and the third brightest in the sky. Alpha Centauri is really a triple star, two of its components form a double star, and the third component is a red dwarf which is 2 degrees away from the others. This red dwarf is 4 light years away from Earth.

Sagittarius or Centaurus, is also home to the brightest and largest globular cluster of stars in the sky. It is called Omega Centauri and it contains more than a million stars.

The Sun enters the star constellation Sagittarius about 22nd November.

Star Sign of Sun Beams – Capricorn!

Capricorn, tenth sign of the Zodiac, is an earth sign and astrologers believe it is ruled by the planet Saturn.

(21 December – 19 January)

In Hindu mythology, Sani was identified with the planet Saturn. Sani was known as the evil-eyed one because his glance could burn anything instantly. Hindus believed that the planets were able to affect the life of the individual and the course of history and for this reason, the planets are especially worshipped in times of danger.

But to the ancient Romans, Saturn was the god of fertility and planting, who, according to their myths, presided over a golden age of happiness and prosperity. The Romans honoured Saturn every year with a festival called Saturnalia. The festival began on December 17th and lasted for seven days.

During this period, schools and businesses closed, no criminals could be prosecuted and no wars could be started. Slaves were given temporary freedom. During the festival of Saturnalia feasts were held and gifts were given. The most popular gifts were wax candles and small clay figures.

Saturn, a gas planet, is the sixth planet nearest the Sun and the second largest planet in our Solar System. Saturn has a large family of at least 18 moons and its rings are made from countless mini moons.

The word Capricorn comes from the Latin 'caper', meaning goat, and 'cornu' meaning horn. Capricorn is symbolised by the goat in the star constellation Capricornus. It is thought that the ancients of Mesopotamia gave the constellation the name of goat because of its position in the sky. It is in that part of the Zodiac which was the place occupied by the Sun at the winter solstice. The constellation having first travelled south from the equator, and then climbing up to meet the Sun. Of course, the goat is a great climber.

The Greeks included the traditional goat in their mythology only they dedicated it to the god Pan. Pan was the god of the countryside and became so powerful that his name came to mean everything. We find his name in the words, 'panarama', 'panacea' and 'pantheism.' He invented the reed pipe known as the panpipe. Pan has the horns and legs of a goat.

Once, while Pan was enjoying the company of the other gods on the banks of a river, the great one hundred headed monster, Typhon appeared to attack them. The divine revellers jumped into the water and took on other shapes. Pan disguised himself as a fish below water, and above the water he took on the shape of a goat. Because he took on that animals shape to save his life, Zeus placed the image of the goat in the sky to form the constellation Capricornus.

The Tropic of Capricorn used to lie directly below this constellation. The Tropic of Capricorn is an imaginary line that traces the southern boundary of Earth's Tropical Zone. It marks the farthest limit south of the equator where the Sun can appear directly overhead.

The vertical rays of the Sun beam down on the Tropic of Capricorn at exactly noon on the day of the winter solstice which is December 21/22.

Capricornus is one of the dimmest star constellations and does not contain many celestial objects, but it does have one globular cluster. It is easy to see Capricornus in September. It lies between Aquarius and Sagittarius.

Cup Bearer of Zeus - Aquarius!

Aquarius, eleventh sign of the Zodiac, is an air sign and astrologers believe it is ruled by two planets, Saturn and Uranus.

(20 January – 19 February)

Saturn, was named after an early god of the Romans who was a god of fertility and planting. The Romans held a feast in his honour, the feast of Saturnalia. Saturnalia, which celebrates the winter equinox, was held originally for only two days, but this was extended to seven, beginning 17th December. Entire communities celebrated, slaves and masters became equals for the week, and rules of conduct were suspended. The festival originated to commemorate the winter planting. However it lost its agricultural significance and became a time of general merriment.

Saturn, a gas planet, is the sixth planet nearest the Sun and the second largest in our Solar System. Saturn has seven thin flat rings around it which are made up of ice particles.

Uranus gets its name from the creation story of the Greeks, where Uranus suddenly came out of Earth who was the goddess Gaea. Gaea herself, the Earth, had come out of Chaos, which came before all things. Uranus was a sky god.

Uranus, seventh major planet of the Solar System, was discovered by William Herschel in 1781. It has 15 moons. From Earth it appears as a smooth greenish disc and in good conditions is just bright enough to be seen by the naked eye. Uranus has a series of eleven narrow rings around it which are not visible from Earth.

Almost all the ancient cultures of the world saw the star constellation of Aquarius as a man with a water pitcher or vase, pouring water down to Earth. The only difference being the choice of receptacle. The old Chaldeans saw it as a watering can, the Chinese called it 'the filled vase', and to the Greeks and Romans, it became 'water pourer' or 'water carrier', eventually being called Aquarius. Aquarius is Latin for 'of water' and used as a noun is 'water carrier'. The Sumerians believed that Aquarius brought on a global flood.

Greek mythology tells its own story of how Aquarius the water carrier originated. It tells how Ganymede, a young and beautiful shepherd, was abducted by Zeus who disguised himself as an eagle. Ganymede was the son of King Tros, whose name was given to the kingdom of Troy.

Ganymede was tending his sheep on Mount Ida when Zeus caught a glimpse of him and was overwhelmed by his beauty. He felt that Ganymede should reside in Olympia, the home of the gods, so he changed into an eagle, swooped down to the craggy slopes of Ida, and carried Ganymede off to serve as cup bearer to the gods.

The position of cup bearer was already filled by Zeus' own daughter Hebe. A competition began between Hebe and Ganymede for the honour of serving the gods. Ganymede won the post and stayed on as the favoured companion of Zeus. Zeus placed the eagle into the skies as the constellation Aquila, and immortalised Ganymede as the constellation Aquarius.

The star constellation Aquarius lies between Pisces and Capricornus and contains the Helix Nebula, the closest planetary nebula to us. One of the oldest constellations in the known Universe, many of the stars in Aquarius have names that refer to good luck.

There are three globular clusters in Aquarius which can be viewed through a telescope. It also contains the planetary nebula, Saturn Nebula, so named because it looks like the planet Saturn when viewed through a telescope.

The Age of Aquarius is an astrological age which is about to begin, marked by the precession of the vernal equinox into Aquarius, believed by some to herald world wide peace and harmony.

The Sun enters Aquarius about the 21st January.

Oceanic Symbol - Pisces!

Pisces, twelfth sign of the Zodiac, is a water sign and astrologers believe it is ruled by the planets Jupiter and Neptune.

(20th February – 20th March)

In Roman mythology, Neptune was the god of the sea who had power over the sea and seafaring, and who could cause storms or prevent them. He was also the god of earthquakes and horses.

The ancient Romans were a seafaring people, so Neptune played an important part in their daily lives. The Romans prayed to Neptune for safe voyages and on their safe return would show their gratitude by dedicating valuable objects to him.

Neptune was the son of Saturn and Ops. He married beautiful Aphrodite, goddess of love, who was created from sea foam. They had a son named Triton, who was half man and half fish. An epic poem written by the Roman poet Virgil, tells how Neptune calms a storm that had threatened to destroy the fleet of the Trojan hero Aeneas. Neptune, Aphrodite and Triton feature in many lovely paintings. Some show Neptune riding a chariot pulled by seahorses and accompanied by dolphins. The planet Neptune was named after this god.

Neptune is the eighth planet from the Sun, is a gas planet, and it was discovered in 1846 using maths. Neptune has at least 18 moons, one of them is named after the son of Neptune, Triton. For 20 years, out of every 248, Pluto swaps places with Neptune as the eighth planet pushing Neptune into ninth place.

Pluto has just completed one of these twenty year terms which began February the 7th, 1979 and ended February the 11th, 1999. Pluto then returned to its ninth place position! Neptune's moon, Titon, is the only moon in the Solar System that orbits in the opposite direction to its planet.

Jupiter, the other planet associated with the star constellation Pisces, is the god of Romans who, according to Roman mythology, was king of the gods and the Universe. Jupiter made certain that mortals lived out their lives according to their fate. Jupiter was also the father of the nine Muses, who inspired art, poetry and learning.

Jupiter is the largest planet in our Solar System and is the second brightest after Venus. A giant, it would take 1,000 Earths to fill its volume! Jupiter has 16 known moons. The largest four are known collectively as Gililean Satellites after Galileo, the Italian astronomer who first discovered them in 1610 with one of the earliest telescopes.

Pisces' symbol of the fish has a particular Greek legend association with it which says that the fish were placed in the skies to form that star constellation after Aphrodite and her son Eos jumped into a river and turned themselves into two fish to escape the monster Typhon.

However, almost every ancient civilisation saw this constellation as the image of the fish. In early pictures of the symbol, two fish are swimming in different directions, with their tails joined by a ribbon. Other ancient representations retain the two fish, but place one above the other.

The symbol of the fish has been traced to an original close connection with the ancient Babylonian calendar, which was based on the moon. The lunar months being shorter than those of the Sun, the calendar could have caused problems which affected the seasonal festivals, so the Babylonians wisely introduced an extra month, a sort of leap year, at the time of the year when the Sun was in that part of the sky that they represented by the fish.

That time of year was the fishing season. They therefore put two fish into the constellation, doubling the image, as well as the month. The star constellation Pisces is a large northern constellation which lacks bright stars. It lies between Aquarius and Aries and contains the spring equinox. The easternmost celestial fish is located just below Andromeda, and the westernmost fish is below Pegasus.

The Sun enters Pisces about the 20th of February.

The Mother of Medicine
Astrology

One of the most important reasons for studying astrology long ago was medicine. Under Greek influence, the scope of astrology was enlarged and, because practically all the known sciences were connected, plants, drugs, and animal life of all kinds were associated with one or another of the stars or planets.

The fate of the individual, led to associating parts of the body with the planets and various systems to help diagnosis and treatment were devised.

The Zodiac was regarded as the prototype of the human body, and the different parts all had their corresponding section in the Zodiac itself. The head was placed between the first sign of the Zodiac, Aries the ram; and the feet in the last sign, Pisces the fishes. Between those two extremes, the other parts were distributed amongst the other signs of the Zodiac.

With human anatomy thus connected with the planets, stars and constellations, medicine became an integral part of astrology. Bloodletting, a medical treatment, was regulated by the position of the moon. When the moon was in the Zodiac ruling a particular part of the body, bloodletting from that part would be avoided since the attraction of the moon could cause excessive bleeding. (Even today, some surgeons consider the phases of the moon before operating.) Medical manuscripts and almanacs included the figure of astronomical man, similar to the above illustration. Astronomical man illustrated the phases of the moon for physicians, thus showing its pulling power.

Students of medicine learned astrology for four years and were instructed to use astronomical tables and almanacs in order to make their prognosis or conduct bloodletting, and to help them to decide when to offer treatment. This practice continued for hundreds of years.

Dr Francis Moore (1657-1715), astrologer, schoolmaster and physician in Lambeth England, published his own almanac in 1699, with the aim of helping farmers to predict the weather. Then, in 1700, expanded it and it re-appeared as Vox Stellaru, The Voice of the Stars, and contained predictions for the next year with astrological abbreviations.

This publication became known as Old Moore's Almanac and new editions appeared annually over the next three hundred years. Dr Moore's black and white publication also combined herbal recipes and remedies with the most favourable astrological times for taking them.

Born the son of a pauper, Dr Moore was self educated and he became an eminent physician and astrologer who served at the court of Charles the 2nd of England. When he died in 1715, his almanac was bought by the London Liveried Stationers Company who sold it to its present publisher, Foulshauns, in the nineteenth century. Now three hundred and ten years old, Old Moore's Almanac continues to be popular today. Dr Moore, and those who went before him, surely were the voice of the stars and that voice was the mother of medicine.

The Pharaohs' Signs of the Zodiac

Introduction to Egyptian Astrology

The Egyptian Temple of Dendera, dedicated to the goddess Hathor is thought to have been constructed by the Ptolemies in the first century BC, on the site of an earlier temple. When re-discovered, in the days of Napoleon, it was found to contain two zodiacs. A rectangular zodiac, and a circular zodiac. The original circular zodiac was removed from the temple's ceiling and is now housed in the museum in Louvre, Paris. Only a plaster copy of it is left in the Temple of Dendera.

The exact age of the two zodiacs is unknown but some have assigned an age of over 15,000 years to them, and others say that these zodiacs represent records that span more than 87, 000 years. More recent excavations, at TombTT353, constructed by Senenmut, confirm that the ancient Egyptians were interested in astrology. Tomb TT353 contains an astrological ceiling within chamber A., leaving no doubt that these ancients had a great knowledge of astronomy too.

It is to Egypt that we owe the twenty four hour day, and many great works from there have contributed to alchemical and astrological thought. For example, the works of a mysterious priest named Nechepso, composed in Alexandria around 150BC, had a profound effect on Renaissance astrologers and were influential on those who combined magic with their astrology, such as John Dee, astrologer to Queen Elizabeth the first. The great library at Alexandria became important to Mediterranean civilisation as a centre of astrological learning after the inclusion of Egypt in the Roman Empire in 30BC.

The Egyptian Government has appealed to France and UNESCO for the return to Egypt of the original circular zodiac taken from the Temple of Dendera, since it is part of that country's heritage. Recently, the Egyptian government encouraged its citizens to consult their own zodiac, as perceived by the Pharoahs, in reference to their astrological star signs.

The following pages are an introduction to the Pharoahs' Star Signs and some of the mythical stories behind them. To find your Egyptian star sign, simply look through the dates on the following pages for your birth date.

The God of Learning

Thoth

(August 29th – September 27th)

People born within this specific date group, are born under the sign of Thoth, according to the Egyptian zodiac. They are capable problem solvers and excellent organisers.

A lunar god, Thoth is often depicted with the head of an ibis, wearing the lunar crescent on his head. He is the creator of magic, the inventor of writing, and the divine record keeper and mediator. According to Egyptian mythology, it is Thoth who questions the souls of the dead about their deeds in life and it is he who is responsible for recording the judgement of those souls, in the Halls of Judgement, where their hearts are weighed against the feather of truth before they pass into the afterlife.

Known too, as a god of wisdom, it is recorded that Thoth is the patron of knowledge, including scientific, medical and mathematical writing. A teacher of man, it was Thoth who gifted mankind the art of hieroglyphic writing. Scrupulously fair, Thoth is also considered to be counsellor to the other Egyptian gods, who often went to him for advice.

Thoth helped the goddess Isis to conceive Horus, by helping Isis to bring back her husband, Osiris, to life, after he was torn apart by his brother, Set. After Horus's conception, Osiris died again and went on to become Lord of the Underworld. To stop Set from killing his new brother Horus, Isis hid the infant in the papyrus and lotus thickets of the Nile delta in Lower Egypt. However, one day, the evil Set, transformed himself into a snake and reached the child unseen. He bit the child, poisoning him, then made a quick getaway. Isis was so distraught, and still in grief for her husband, that she could not get her own powers to work to help Horus, or to bring him back. She cried out to the other gods and Ra, hearing the goddess, sent Thoth to find out what had happened. Thoth worked great magic and the poison was driven out of Horus's body, bringing the baby back to life. Thoth then ordered the people of the marshes and all birds and animals who lived there to keep watch over them.

Worshipped widely throughout Egypt from circa 3000BC until the end of ancient Egyptian history, circa 400AD, Thoth's cult centre was Hermopolis.

The God of the Shining Sun

Horus

(September 28th – October 27th)

Those born under this sign would risk their lives to avenge their father's death; would courageously face dangers; are brilliantly sociable and motivated to win the best in life, according the Egyptian astrology.

Horus, the god of the shining sun, is also patron of the living Pharaoh, young men, light, war and rulers, and many others depending on his variant.

Most commonly depicted as a falcon headed man, Horus is also know as a falcon, a lion with the head of a falcon, or a sphinx. Whatever form he takes, Horus is regarded as a prince amongst the gods and specifically associated as the protector of the living Pharaoh. Sometimes he is shown as a falcon resting on the neck of the Pharaoh, spreading his wings to either side of the Pharaoh's head, whispering guidance in his ear.

Egyptian tradition states that Horus is one of the most universally important of the gods and that he was born at Kempis in the Nile delta. His father was the dead Osiris and his mother was Isis. He avenged his father's death by regaining the throne from his brother Seth after an 80-year struggle and became the first ruler of all Egypt. Legend states that the evil Set or Seth, tore out Horus's eye, which was later restored by his mother, Isis. This incident brought about the symbol representing kingship, perfection and protection against evil influence, that is 'The Eye of Horus'.

The mythical Horus is described as a celestial falcon whose right eye was the sun and left eye the moon. The speckled feathers on his breast were considered to be the stars. His glorious wings were the sky that created the wind. In this form, Horus was worshipped at Nekhen where he was assimilated with a number of other local falcon gods. A patron of the Nekhem monarchy, Horus was the first known National god.

Worshipped throughout Egypt, Horus's variant forms were widespread.

The Goddess of the Royal Cobra

Wadget

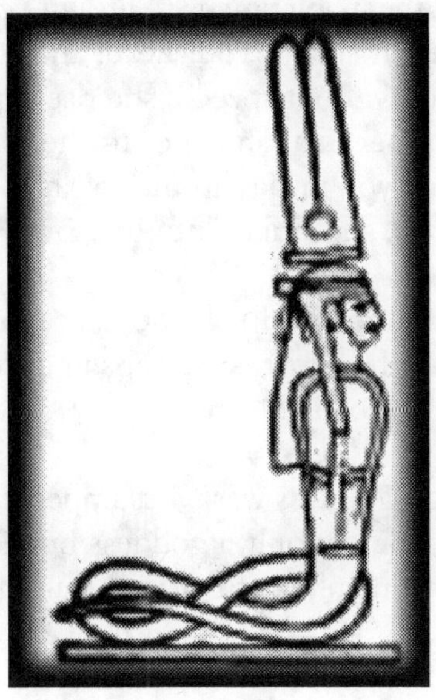

(October 28th – November 26th)

According to Egyptian astrology, those born under this sign are rational, cautious, conscientious, altruistic, ambitious and self-opinionated. They are also said to be strongly loyal to family values.

Wadjet, who takes the forms of a fire breathing cobra, a winged cobra, and a woman headed cobra, was the goddess of a city who grew to become the goddess of Lower Egypt. She is one of two ladies, (twinned with the vulture goddess of Upper Egypt, Nekhbet), responsible for the guardianship of the whole of Egypt. These two were known as 'nebty', the two ladies of the Pharaoh.

The symbol of the sacred serpent, Wadjet is the emblem of power worn on the headdress of ancient Egyptian divinities and sovereigns. A goddess of royal authority, she forms an integral part of the symbolism of the sun god Ra, coiling round the sun-disc.

According to mythology, Wadjet created the papyrus swamps of the delta, was a wet nurse to the god Horus, and is the mother of the god of the primeval lotus blossom, Neferturn.

According to 'The Book of the Dead', the goddess Wadjet comes to you in the form of the living uraeus to anoint your head with her flames. She rises up on the left side of your head, and she shines from the right side of your temples without speech; she rises up on your head during each hour of the day, even as she does for her father Ra, and through her, the terror which you inspire in the spirits is increased. She will never leave you, and of you, she strikes into the souls, which are made perfect.

Compassionate too, Wadjet helped Isis nurse young Horus as well as help hide them in the papyrus swamps in order to keep them safe from Set who wanted to kill Horus.

This protection goddess was worshipped at the Temple of Wadjet and was believed to be not only a goddess but also part of the land of Egypt itself. Her main cult centre was at Buto, in the Nile delta.

The Mighty One – Lady of Heaven
Sekhmet

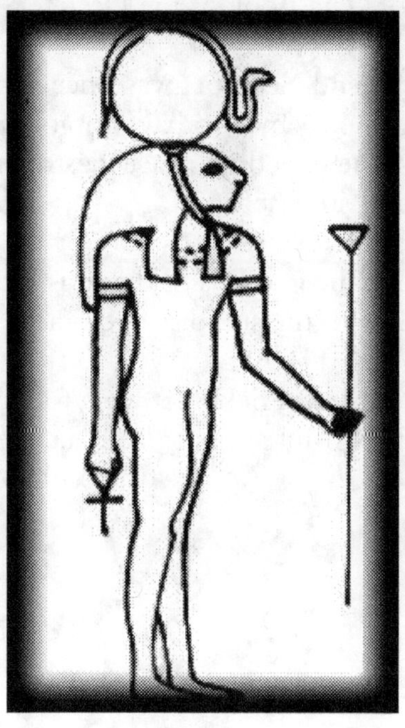

(November 27th – December 26th)

According to the Pharaoh's signs of the zodiac, those born under this sign possess a brilliant mentality, have sustained optimism, and great imagination.

One of the most powerful of the Egyptian goddesses, Sekhmet is the lion-headed goddess. Associated with war and retribution, she was said to use arrows to pierce her enemies with fire, her breath being the hot desert wind as her body took on the glare of the midday sun. Sekhmet was the goddess who meted out divine punishment to the enemies of the gods and the Pharaohs. She could send out plagues and diseases to enemies and accompanied the Pharaoh into battle.

However, she was also a mother of Nefertem who was a healing god and this protective side to her ensured that Sekhmet was also known as a goddess of healing and surgery. Her priests were specialists in the field of medicine, arts linked to magic and ritual. They were trained surgeons of a remarkable calibre. Sekhmet is mentioned a number of times in the spells of 'The Book of the Dead'.

According to legend, Sekhmet was once sent to Earth by Ra to take vengeance on man who seemed to have forgotten him. So intent on fulfilling his wishes, she ended up nearly destroying the entire human race and Ra himself had to stop her!

A solar goddess, the goddess Sekhmet is most often depicted as a lion-headed woman with the sun disc and uraeus serpent headdress.

Hundreds of statues of Sekhmet were found in the Theban temple precinct of the goddess Mut at South Karnak. Sechmet's cult centre was at Memphis.

The Treasure Guardian
Sphinx

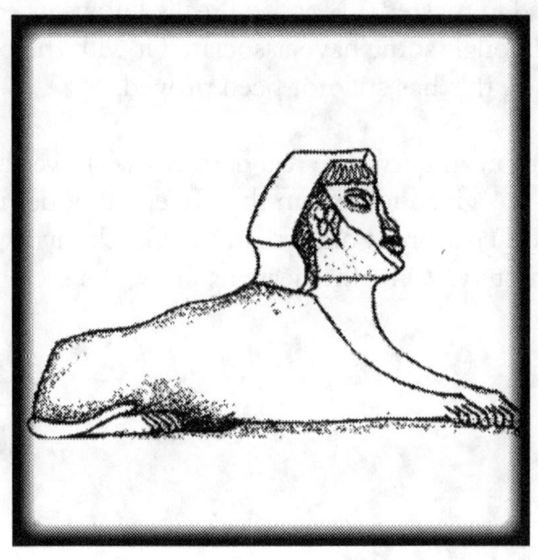

(December 27th – January 25th)

Those born under this sign can, according to Egyptian tradition, change their attitudes to fit nearly all situations. They are stern and shrewd with good self-discipline and high sensibility.

According to mythology, originating in Egypt, the Sphinx is the treasure guardian who could convert himself into the shape of any creature. A shape shifter. Usually depicted with a lions body and a man's head, the most famous example of a Sphinx is perhaps the colossal stone figure which stands prominently amongst the funerary monuments of the Pharaoh Khafra or Chephren, sited on the Giza plateau on the west bank of the Nile River. This guardian Sphinx is thought to show the face of Pharaoh Khafra.

Other famous Egyptian Sphinxes include the alabaster Sphinx of Memphis, and the ram headed Sphinxes representing the god Amun, that line either side of the three kilometre route linking the complexes of the Luxor temple and Karnak in Luxor, (ancient Thebes), of which there were originally nine hundred.

The wonderful Sphinx, guardian of temples, treasure and Pharaohs, is still shrouded in mystery. Non-one really knows its origins, or its secrets, and although some have associated it with the constellations Leo of ancient times, this has still not been proved.

We do not even know the real name of what we call the Sphinx. Its present name was given to it from the Greek in modern times, but this ancient mythical creature is older than the Greek myths and time has only added to its mystery. Only the heavens know the secret of the Sphinx.

The God of Air

Shu

(January 26th – February 24th)

People born under this Pharaoh sign are said to be incredibly creative. Extremely talented, their success is inevitable. Nevertheless, they are always apprehensive of failure.

The god Shu was believed by ancient Egyptians to be the breath of life and Lord of the Air and the upper sky. According to Egyptian mythology, Shu was related to the sun, an aspect of sunlight. One of the protector gods of Ra, on his journey through the underworld, Shu used magic spells to ward off Ra's enemy, the snake demon Apep. Shu is depicted as a man wearing an ostrich feather headdress, holding a sceptre and the ankh sign of life.

As god of the wind, people invoked Shu to give good wind to the sails of boats. He was also called to 'lift up' the spirits of the dead so that they may reach the star lit land or 'light land', reached by means of a great divine ladder that Shu held up.

God of the atmosphere, and the space between the sky and the Earth, Shu was Egypt's second divine ruler, and one of the first deities to be created by Atum.

Shu was considered a god related to living, allowing life to flourish in old Egypt. To the Egyptians, if there was no Shu, there would be no life, and therefore, no Egypt.

Shu was the father of the god Geb and the sky goddess, Nut, and he is frequently depicted in human form standing over Geb and holding Nut aloft with his raised arms.

Queen of the Gods

Isis

(February 25ᵗʰ – March 26ᵗʰ)

Those born within this group of dates are said to be honourable, straightforward and idealistic. Active and self confident, people born under this Egyptian sign use logic and intuition to view things from different perspectives.

Isis must be one of the most or at least, longest, worshipped goddesses. Her worship originated in Africa, spread to ancient Egypt, then her fame spread through the ancient world by the Greeks. The Romans worshipped her in all corners of their empire, and there was even an Isis temple on the River Thames in London. One of the last of the old faiths to die out, the last recorded festival was held in Rome in 394AD.

To the Egyptians though, she was the purest example of

motherhood, loving, clever, loyal and brave. They loved, worshipped and cherished their fruitful goddess, Isis. Isis was also a great magician, and she became one of the most powerful magicians in Egypt when she managed to trick Ra into revealing his secret name to her.

Her heavenly symbol was the star Sirius, the star that marked the beginning of not only the Egyptian New Year, but also the inundation of the Nile.

Isis became a goddess of limitless attributes, a goddess of water, corn, stars, wind, motherhood, and a goddess of the underworld.

A winged goddess, Isis travelled widely. The Kite was sacred to her and she could turn herself into this bird at will. She brought the heavenly scent with her through the land leaving flowers and spices in her wake.

In Egyptian art, Isis is depicted as both human and divine. As a goddess, she took on the headdress of the cow's horns with the sun between them. As a woman, she was shown with the queen's headdress, with the sacred serpent on her forehead.

Her cult originated at Per-hebet and spread throughout Egypt and beyond, and her festivals were many. Originally depicted as a black goddess, identifying her African origin, Isis evolved to suit many cultures and worshipers worldwide. Today, she still has followers.

Lord of Eternity

Osiris

(March 27th – April 25th)

People born under this sign, the sign related to the god of the underworld, are said to be emotionally perplexing and often misunderstood. They can, however, be dynamic, intelligent, and always take up opportunities.

According to Egyptian mythology, Osiris was born in five days and a voice was heard proclaiming that the land of creation was born. He apparently became a king of Egypt, taught men husbandry, established a code of laws, and made men worship the gods. But once, when he returned from instructing other nations of the world, Typhon, the Egyptian Set, and seventy-two of his comrades, captured Osiris. They forced him into a chest and cast the locked chest into the Nile. His wife, Isis, searched until she found the chest at Bablos, where the sea had carried it up and placed it among the branches of the Tamarisk tree. The tree enclosed it within its trunk and there it remained until the tree was cut down and its trunk was taken to become a pillar in the palace of the king of that country.

Isis told the country's queen of her search and was allowed to retrieve the chest and her husband's body, and she returned with them to Egypt. However Typhon found the chest and knowing of Isis' great reputation as a magician, tore Osiris body into fourteen pieces which he scattered up and down throughout the land.

Osiris' loving wife Isis, took a boat made of papyrus and searched until she found every piece of Osiris's body and she built a tomb over each piece. Osiris returned from the other world and taught his son Horus the use of arms. Eventually, Horus defeated Typhus/Set, and avenged his father's death.

Ancient Egyptians believed Osiris was the son of a god who lived a good life upon Earth as a wise and just king. When Osiris obtained a new life in the other world, they believed that he reigned there as god and king. To the Egyptians, Osiris was the god's son who suffered, and died, and rose again to reign eternally in heaven.

A cult of Osiris was widespread about 3500BC and text at the temple of Dendera describes that a number of festivals in his name were celebrated during the month of Khoak at chief sanctuaries around Egypt. Worshipped throughout Egypt, Osiris' cult centre was Abydos.

The God who Constructed the World
Amun

(April 26th – May 25th)

People born under this sign are thought to be strong, firm, and always sought for guidance. They are excellent leaders with outstanding courage and self-confidence, according to the pharaoh's zodiac.

To the ancient Egyptians, Amun was the god who constructed the world. Their creator god. As he became more significant, Amun was assigned a wife. His wife, known as Mut in the areas where Amun was worshipped, was considered to be the divine mother from which the cosmos emerged. So holy, and so independent of the created universe, was Amun, that he could not be seen. As divinity revealed, he was known as Amun-Ra. Ra or Re means, sun.

According to Egyptian mythology, Amun could regenerate himself by becoming a snake and shedding his skin, at Thebes he was revered as a snake deity.

He is portrayed as a pharaoh, with blue skin, wearing a turban surmounted by two tall plumes of feathers, symbolic of dominance over both Lower and Upper Egypt. In this capacity, relating to kingship, Amun was viewed as upholding the rights to justice of the poor, and as a protector of those who travelled in his name. As King of Gods, the Greeks who visited Egypt identified Amun as on a par with Zeus.

As Amun's cult grew widespread, and his identities became merged with the sun god Ra, he became known too as the father of Shu and Tefnut. The Pharaoh Amenhotep the 4th, persecuted the worship of Amun and erased the god's name from monuments, preferring to encourage the worship of the sun itself. However, when Amenhotep died, all his changes were undone by priests and the worship of Amun-Ra was restored.

Although Amun's cult eventually declined in Upper and Lower Egypt, in Nubia, Amun was greatly honoured and there he remained a national god with priesthoods at Meroe and Nobatia. In Libya, there was an oracle of Amun in the desert at the oasis of Siwa. Alexander the Great journeyed there after the battle of Issus, to be acknowledged the son of the god.

The cult of Amun was linked with Jupiter and his centre was at Thebes.

The Goddess of the Earth and the Sky
Hathor

(May 26th – June 24th)

Those born under this sign of the Egyptian zodiac are said to enjoy life to the full and win the best in most situations. They are charming and romantic, excellent communicators and have strong connections with the arts.

The goddess Hathor was associated with the great queens of Egypt and she is also seen as the incarnation of dance. Stories were told of how Hathor danced to cheer up Ra, the sun god, when he was in despair.

A mother goddess, Hathor's cult was exceptional in that both men and women were her priests and because Hathor was patron of inspiration and arts, most of her followers and priests were artisans, musicians and dancers. Using their blessed talents, Hathor's worshipers created rituals to her that were works of art.

In Egyptian mythology, Hathor was originally a personification of The Milky Way, which was then seen as the milk that flowed from the udders of a heavenly cow. Worshipped during the 2nd dynasty, some say that Hathor was even worshipped by the Scorpion King. The Milky Way was seen as a waterway in the heavens, sailed upon by both the sun god Ra, and the king, leading Egyptians to call it 'The Nile in the Sky'. Hathor was identified as responsible for the yearly inundation of the Nile.

Hathor has many representations. In the Hathor temple, dedicated to her worship, is a representation of an electric lamp which some say associates Hathor as a light deity.

In art, Hathor is sometimes depicted as a golden cow, crowned with stars, or as a woman with the ears of a cow and headdress of horns holding the sun disc. This depiction is associated with divine motherhood and sometimes the pharaoh is depicted standing beside her as a calf.

Any seven depictions of her; seven being the mystical number of the known planets at that time; were considered special if gathered together. These 'Seven Hathors' were said to disguise themselves as young women, and attend the birth of a child. Then, one by one, each would announce aspects of the child's fate. The Pleiades later represented this aspect of Hathor.

Worshipped throughout Egypt, Hathor's cult centre was at Dendera, in Upper Egypt.

Symbol of Purity

Bennu/Phoenix

(June 25th to July 24th)

According to the Egyptian pharaoh's signs of the zodiac, those born under this sign can create possibilities from scratch. They are said to be optimistic, flexible, and can promote optimism in others. They are also often thought of as dreamers.

The Bennu bird is said to have flown over the waters of Num at the time of original creation. Like the sun god, Bennu was self-generating and was believed to rise constantly renewed, like the sun, each morning. Eventually, Bennu lived a long life before renewal.

A story from Herodotus tells how this bird lived 500 years before building a nest of aromatic boughs and spices which it then set ablaze and was then consumed within the inferno. From this, a new Bennu emerged, embalmed the ashes of its father, and then flew with them to lay them on the altar of the temple of Ra or Re. However, in the mythology of the pharaohs, the bird never dies.

Connected with Ra, the hieroglyphic sign depicting the bird was used to write the name of the sun god and was said to be Ra's soul. Known as the mythical phoenix of Egypt, the Bennu bird was associated with the rising of the Nile and resurrection.

The Egyptians knew that months do not correspond to lunar months, and that years do not correspond to solar years. They calculated their seasonal years by the stars to be the time between successive helical risings of the star Sirius. Representing creation and renewal, Bennu was connected to the Egyptian calendar and The Temple of Bennu was known for its time keeping devices. Known as the "Wandering Year", the Egyptian Calendar had a year that was 365 days long; had 12 months of 30 days each (divided into 3 weeks of 10 days), with 5 days at the end of each year. Already used throughout antiquity, this calendar was used by astronomers in the Middle Ages because of its mathematical regularity.

Egyptian myths say that the Bennu bird created itself from a fire that was burned in a holy tree. Bennu, it was said, rested on a sacred pillar known as the benben stone. Some priests considered this pillar the most holy place on Earth. When carved on the back of the heart scarab, and buried with the dead, the Bennu bird is said to be the symbol of re-birth in the netherworld.

In Egyptian art, the Bennu is depicted as a grey, purple, blue, or white heron with a long beak and a two-feathered crest. Sometimes, Bennu is depicted as a yellow wagtail or as an eagle with feathers of red and gold.

He Who is Upon the Mountain

Anubis

(July 25th – August 28th)

The sign of Anubis is the most determined of all signs. Those born under this sign are thought to be self-confident, and their ability to keep things under control makes them widely respected. They are also sympathetic, generous, loving and perseverant in proving their viewpoint.

Anubis is an incredibly ancient god and was the original god of the underworld before Osiris took over. He is often depicted as a man with the head of a Jackal like animal. Unlike a real Jackal, Anubis' head is black, representing his position as a god of the dead. He protected the dead as they journeyed through the underworld, conducting them, testing their knowledge of the gods and faith, and it was Anubis who placed their hearts on the Scales of Justice during the Judging of the Heart ceremony.

The Egyptians believed it was Anubis who kept watch, from the mountains, over the ancient tombs and graves, ready to rush down and protect the deceased from desecration, protecting their souls and eternal-resting place.

As the god of embalming, Anubis became associated with the as yet, mysterious imiut fetish, where a stuffed, headless animal skin, often a feline or bull, tied to a pole, was present in funerary rites. The origins of this fetish are unknown at the present time.

Ancient Egyptian texts say that Anubis, like a Jackal, walked silently through the shadows of life and death and lurked in dark places, watchful by day as well as by night.

Images of Anubis as a seated Jackal above nine prisoners were stamped on many of the seals to tombs in the Valley of the Kings, symbolising Anubis' protection against thieves and evil doers who entered the necropolis.

In later times, Anubis was identified as the Greek god Hermes, becoming Hermanubis. Worshipped throughout Egypt, Anubis' cult centre was in Cynopolis. Worship of this god continued at least up to the 2nd century and the name Hermanubis appears in the alchemical and hermetical literature of the Middle Ages and the Renaissance.

The Jade Emperor's Zodiac

China's Animal Signs

Introduction

The western zodiac was known in China by the 17th century AD, but early Chinese astrologers did not use the ecliptic stars, (those that represent the course of the sun through the year, divided among the twelve zodiac constellations, with a measurement of 30 degrees to each division). The ancient Chinese astrologers used the circumpolar stars.

The old Chinese Empire saw itself as the counterpart of the Middle Kingdom of Heaven – the region of stars that never set. The circumpolar stars are seen all year round. The Emperor, representing the Pole Star, sat facing south to give an audience, and his astrologers used an old system, known as the system of the Four Palaces. Later, the ecliptic was included in Chinese astrology and this was given the name of The Yellow Road, in opposition to the equator, which, to the Chinese is The Red Road.

There are several stories relating to how the twelve animals of the Chinese zodiac were chosen. According to one legend, the Jade

Emperor, although having ruled Heaven and Earth justly and wisely for many years, had never had the time to visit Earth personally. He grew curious as to what the creatures of earth looked like, so he charged his chief advisor with selecting the twelve most interesting animals and bringing them to Heaven to satisfy his curiosity.

The Emperor's advisor sent invitations to the rat, cat, ox, tiger, rabbit, dragon, snake, horse, ram, monkey, chicken, and the dog. The cat asked the rat if he would mind waking him up on the day they were all to visit Heaven so that he would not oversleep. The rat, worrying that he would seem ugly compared to the cat, did not wake it. The cat missed the meeting with the Jade Emperor and was replaced by the pig. The cat never forgave the rat and these two creatures have been enemies ever since. Another story says rat pushed the cat into the water while the animals raced across the river. Cat and rat were both riding on the back of the Ox as it swam the river. Whatever the true story, the Emperor Jade was so pleased with the animals he met that he decided to divide the years amongst them and he chose the twelve for the zodiac.

The Jade Emperor is known by children and others and Grandpa Heaven and formally as the Pure August and Jade Emperor. He is the ruler of Heaven according to Chinese mythology and from the 9th century he became patron deity of the Chinese imperial family.

The most important of the Chinese Daoist pantheon, the Jade Emperor and his court are part of a celestial bureaucracy, mirroring that of ancient China, who rule over every aspect of human and animal life.

Today, Chinese astrology has spread world-wide with the migration of the Chinese and it is beginning to have an impact on the thought of western astrologers. A crater on Saturn's moon, Rhea, discovered by the Voyager 2 spacecraft was named after the Jade Emperor.

Chinese tradition follows the Chinese calendar thought to have been invented by the Emperor Huangdi, nearly 3000 years ago. The Chinese New Year and important festivals are celebrated according to the ancient calendar, which is based entirely on the astronomical movement of the Sun, Moon and Stars.

In the Chinese Calendar, the year has 12 months and a leap year 13. An ordinary year has 353, 354 or 355 days and a leap year has 383, 384, or 385 days. Leap years are determined by counting the number of the new moons between the eleventh month in one year and the eleventh month of the next year. If there are 13 full moons, then a leap month must be inserted.

The Chinese calendar doesn't count the years continuously. It works in 60 year cycles and each year has a name made up of two parts. The first part is the Heavenly stem, and the second part is an Earthly branch.

Each of the twelve animals chosen for the Emperor Jade's zodiac is associated with certain personality traits. The characteristics of the animal associated with the year of ones birth are influenced by what time of the day one is born, what fixed element one belongs to, as well as the influence of Yin and Yang. Yin and Yang are eternal opposites. Yin (black), represents Winter, night and transition, and Yang (white), represents Summer, day, birth and light. The five elements are Wood, Fire, Earth, Metal and Water, and these influence each animal sign. To find out more about the individual animal signs of the zodiac, and the one relating to your birth date, look up your birth year in the following pages.

Chinese Zodiac

Birth Years 1924, 1936, 1948, 1972, 1984, 1996, 2008

The Rat

People born under this Chinese sign, according to Chinese astrologers, are creative, honest, generous, ambitious, and can be wasteful.

Out of the twelve animals of the Chinese Zodiac, Rats get on best with Monkeys and Dragons, but not so well with Horses.

A symbol of good luck and wealth, this sign is motivated by its own interests, can adapt to most environments easily, and is very family orientated. Although they may set their targets too high whilst young, people born under the sign of the Rat become more realistic as time goes by and can eventually achieve their life goals and find true happiness.

In Chinese mythology, it was the Rat who was given the task of inviting the animals to report to the Jade Emperor to be selected for the zodiac signs. One legend states that Rat forgot to invite the Cat, who never forgave him. Another states that the cat finished too late, coming thirteenth in place, due to the Rat pushing him into a river that the animals had to race across. The Cat vowed to be the enemy of the Rat forever more.

Chinese Zodiac

Birth Years 1937, 1949, 1961, 1973, 1985, 1997, 2009

The Ox

According to Chinese astrology, people born under this Chinese sign are powerful and faithful individuals of good leadership who look before they leap.

Capable and hardworking, Ox people can be a little moody and stubborn. To those who are important to them, however, they can be very loving, gentle and supportive.

Out of the twelve animals of the Chinese Zodiac, the Ox gets on best with Snakes and Roosters, though not so well with Goats.

Capable and hardworking, Ox people are determined in everything they do and steadfast.

According to legend, when the animals had to race across a river to win a place in the Chinese zodiac, Ox was very worried about his poor eyesight when first he contemplated swimming across the river. However, he took the plunge and swam determinedly. So focussed was Ox on getting to the other side, he never noticed that the Rat had jumped on his back. Ox swam so strongly that he reached the shore before all the other animals, but Rat sprang from his back and landed ashore first, placing Ox in the second position of the zodiac.

Another legend tells that Ox was originally a servant of the Heavenly Palace. He volunteered to sow seeds for the herders on Earth

who didn't have enough grass to feed their animals. But he fell, and
scattered the seeds everywhere so the farmers couldn't grow their grain.
He was thrown out of Heaven so, to make amends, he set forth to eat all
the grass that wasn't needed. As he paid his debt and all was now well,
the Jade Emperor made him second of the chosen animals.

Chinese Zodiac

Birth Years 1938, 1950, 1962, 1974, 1986, 1998, 2010

The Tiger

People who are born under this Chinese sign of the zodiac are said to be born leaders, are magnetically charming, and fun to be around, according to Chinese astrologers. Tiger people can be noble and warm-hearted too.

Out of the twelve animals of the Chinese Zodiac, Tigers get on best with Horses and Dogs.

A symbol of great courage, Tigers are not afraid to go it alone, and will fight to the bitter end if a cause is worthy. However, they can react badly to stress and tend to have mood swings. Once Tigers find direction, they accomplish much in life and happiness.

Originally, according to legend, Tiger was the guard of Heaven and was sent down to Earth to control the other animals who were causing havoc. After many great battles, the Jade Emperor rewarded him by making him the king of all animals and marking his skin with one stroke for every animal he had defeated.

The Emperor replaced the Lion with the Tiger as third of the chosen animals because Lion had caused disturbances on Earth.

Chinese Zodiac

Birth Years 1939, 1951, 1963, 1975, 1987, 1999, 2011

The Rabbit

According to Chinese astrologers, people born under this sign of the Chinese zodiac are quiet, reserved, retrospective and thoughtful. A sensitive sign, Rabbit people give very much of themselves. Their discerning natures and hard won assertiveness ensures that people born under this sign will go far.

Rabbits are very popular and have a wide circle of friends and family. Compassionate in nature, Rabbit people are said to be very protective of those they hold dear. Rabbits detest conflict and will avoid it at any cost, which sometimes means that they don't face up to their problems.

Of the twelve chosen animals of the Chinese zodiac, Rabbits get on best with Goats/Sheep, and Pigs.

On the day of choosing the twelve animals at the Heavenly Palace, according to legend, the Jade Emperor decided to have a race for some positions. Rabbit was so far ahead of the rest of the animals, that he decided to stop and have a nap. Whilst sleeping, he was overtaken by the Rat, the Ox, and the Tiger.

Consequently, the Emperor made him fourth of the twelve animals. Bitter at not being first, the Rabbit moved his home underground where his descendants live to this day.

Chinese Zodiac

Birth Years 1928, 1940, 1952, 1964, 1976, 1988, 2000

The Dragon

Dragon people, according to Chinese astrology, are considered to be the most eccentric in the Chinese zodiac. Those born under this sign are idealists, perfectionists, and born thinking they are perfect. An aggressive and determined sign, Dragons will go after what they want, and generally succeed in getting it.

Of the twelve animals of the Chinese zodiac, Dragons get on best with Rats and Monkeys.

To Chinese people, this is the most popular animal in the zodiac and during the Year of the Dragon, there is a noticeable rise in the birth rates in China.

Dragon people are said to be capable of such deep sincerity and openness, that they can disarm the most explosive of situations.

On the day of choosing the twelve animal signs, according to legend, The Jade Emperor thought that the Dragon and the Tiger both looked awesome and ferocious, so he decided to make the Dragon king of the water and the Tiger, king of the Earth. As Tiger was already a sign, the Dragon was given the same status making him the fifth of the chosen twelve animals.

Chinese Zodiac

Birth Years 1929, 1941, 1953, 1965, 1977, 1989, 2001

The Snake

People born under this sign of the Chinese zodiac, according to Chinese astrologers, are great thinkers and can be psychic. The Snake is considered an enigma in the Chinese zodiac.

Of the twelve chosen animals of the Chinese zodiac, Snakes get on best with the Ox, Dragon and the Rabbit.

Rich in wisdom and charm, Snake people are said to be guided by their intuition and deep thoughts.

According to Chinese mythology, the Snake once had legs, but he was lazy and relied on the Frog, who didn't have legs, to catch his food. The Frog was popular and the snake grew resentful, and began biting, even killing, other creatures. He was summoned before the Jade Emperor and, as a punishment; his legs were taken from him and were given to the Frog.

Ashamed by his behaviour, the Snake set about redeeming himself by helping Dragon control the rains and donating his body to science. The Emperor was so impressed that he made the Snake the sixth of the twelve chosen animals

Chinese Zodiac

Birth Years 1930, 1942, 1954, 1966, 1978, 1990, 2002

The Horse

Those born under this sign of the Chinese zodiac are very independent, intelligent and friendly, with a capacity for hard work that is amazing, according to Chinese astrologers. Horse people are also very adventurous and free-spirited.

Of the twelve chosen animals of the Chinese zodiac, Horses get on best with the Tiger, the Sheep/Goat, and the Dog.

Horse people love both physical and mental stimulation and are skilful both in business and love. They are also thought to be dedicated to every task.

When the Horse was still in Heaven, according to Chinese mythology, he had a magnificent pair of wings, but he became arrogant and a bully. One day, he got angry and kicked a guard and killed him. The Jade Emperor was so furious that he ordered that the horse's wings be cut off and that he should be placed under a great mountain.

The Horse wanted to make amends so he dedicated his life to serving humanity by ploughing fields, transporting goods and people, and fighting in battle. The people recommended the Horse be chosen as the seventh of the twelve animals, and he was.

Chinese Zodiac

Birth Years 1931, 1943, 1955, 1967, 1979, 1991, 2003

The Sheep

This is the most feminine sign of the Chinese zodiac, and people of this sign are loved for their gentle and compassionate ways, according to Chinese astrologers. The Sheep can be charming company and Sheep people can be elegant and artistic.

Of the twelve of the chosen animals of the Chinese zodiac, Sheep are happiest in the company of Tiger, Horse, Monkey, Pig, Rabbit, Snake and Dragon.

Sheep people, according to Chinese tradition, are known as good Samaritans and are great team mates.

When the Sheep was still in Heaven, he saw that the people of Earth hadn't enough crops to feed themselves. So, according to legend, Sheep decided to steal some seeds of plentiful from Heaven and sow them on Earth. The Jade Emperor was angry that the Sheep had done this without permission that he ordered that the Sheep be slain and fed to the people.

Every year, new Sheep appeared on Earth as food, and, the grateful people put pressure on the Emperor to make the Sheep the eighth animal of the chosen twelve. This was done.

Birth Years 1932, 1944, 1956, 1968, 1980, 1992, 2004

The Monkey

Those who are born under this sign, are said to be very clever. According to Chinese astrology, Monkey people have extraordinary natures and magnetic personalities.

Of the twelve chosen animals of the Chinese zodiac, Monkey gets on best with Rat, Dragon, Pig, Sheep, Ox, Rabbit, Snake and Dog.

The Monkey is the sign of the inventor, the improviser, and the strongest motivator of the Chinese zodiac. Monkey people, it is said, can master anything under the sun.

Once, according to mythology, Monkey was Tiger's only friend. One day, Tiger got caught in a hunter's net and when the Monkey heard his friend's cries for help, he quickly went to his aid and untied the ropes to free him from the net. Tiger gratefully realised he was indebted to Monkey and so, when the Jade Emperor was considering what place each animal of the twelve should have, Tiger praised Monkey's intelligence and ability, thus ensuring that he was one of the chosen animals and Monkey was placed in the ninth position.

Chinese Zodiac

Birth Years 1933, 1945, 1957, 1969, 1981, 1993, 2005

The Rooster

The Rooster, although definite in decision, can also be a dreamer, according to Chinese astrology. Born under this sign, people are said to be hard workers, good travellers, and are sometimes a little boastful. Rooster people are also said to be friendly, pleasant and obliging.

Of the twelve chosen animals of the Chinese zodiac, Rooster gets on best with Snake, Horse, Rat, Dragon, Pig and Sheep.

With the ability to take things as they come, it is said that Rooster people are very relaxed, or appear so. They can also be neat, precise, direct and organised. However, sometimes, Roosters can be critical in nature, to the point of brutality.

According to Chinese tradition, Rooster was originally so aggressive that he never thought he stood a chance to be chosen by the Jade Emperor. But he helped people on Earth to wake up in the morning by calling out to the sun and this service to humanity led the people to ask the Emperor to consider Rooster.

After a race to help him decide what place to give the Rooster, the Emperor was impressed by the Rooster beating the Dog, and put him in the tenth position.

Chinese Zodiac
Birth Years 1934, 1946, 1958, 1970, 1982, 1994, 2006

The Dog

According to Chinese astrology, those born under this sign will never let you down. The Dog is honest and faithful to those it loves, and people born under this sign are thought to have a strong sense of justice. Integrity means the world to Dog people and their friendships will last a lifetime.

Of the chosen animals of the Chinese zodiac, Dog gets on best with Horse, Pig, Tiger and Monkey.

In ancient times, according to Chinese legend, when the Jade Emperor was choosing the twelve animals for the zodiac, he couldn't make his mind up between the dog and the cat because both served humanity equally. He decided upon a race but the Cat was so scared it ran behind the Pig, so Dog was the eleventh of the twelve animals chosen.

2006 was the Year of the Dog astrologers predict that we will be more idealistic in our views in this year and shed some materialism due to charitable acts. The ever watchful Dog is a sentry ready to defend but the Dog's unselfishness will predispose us to be more big hearted than usual and the Dog's year will lend integrity to our intentions making us act in good faith. Nothing should concern us as long as we stick to the path of righteousness.

The Pig/Boar

The sign of the Pig symbolises the perfect companion and those born under this sign are said to be intellectuals who like to set difficult goals and carry them out. According to Chinese astrology, Pig people are sincere, tolerant, and honest, and just a little naïve sometimes.

Of the twelve chosen animals of the Chinese zodiac, the Pig gets on best with Sheep, Rabbit, Dog and Tiger.

Faith and strength of character keep those born under this animal sign going and Pigs are cultured, caring and very lucky.

According to Chinese mythology, there once lived a rich man who tried desperately to have a son to carry on the family line. Eventually, although old, his prayers were answered. The boy was very spoiled and after his father's death, he squandered his entire inheritance and ended up with no friends and died in poverty.

When he arrived in Heaven, the boy complained to the Jade Emperor that life had treated him unfairly. The Emperor decided that this son had wasted his destiny of good fortune and should be punished so he ordered that the boy should be reborn as a Pig. The Heavenly Officer in charge, misheard the order, and thought that the Emperor said to make the Pig an animal sign of the zodiac. So the young man became reborn as a Pig and was also the last of the chosen twelve animals.

Zodiac of the Sky World

The Eternal Dreamtime

An Introduction to
Aboriginal Cosmology

All space and all time, everything and every living creature or plant, according to Aboriginal Cosmology is both connected and independent, and all are kin. The oldest living culture in the world, the Australian Aboriginal people have carried the spark of their ancestors within them, in an unbroken link, from 'the time before time' or the 'time of the creation of all things', known as Dreamtime, to the present time, for over 50,000 years.

The Ancestor Spirits of the Aboriginals came to Earth in human and other forms, and the land, plants and animals were given their forms as we know them today. These Spirits brought about relationships between groups and individuals, whether people or animals and where they travelled across the land, or stopped, they created rivers, hills and other natural things. When the work of the Ancestor Spirits was over, they changed into animals, stars, hills, trees and rocks.

Oral tradition has passed the stories of those Ancestor Spirits' original places and activities, down through the ages to the present. The stories are an integral part of an indigenous person's 'Dreaming'. For them, the past does not exist, and is alive and well today, and will continue into the future. Dreamtime is eternal. Dreaming stories explain the natural environment and cover many themes and topics. They tell how things were created, where languages came from, how fire was first used, even about the arrival of the first Europeans. The Dreamtime or Dreaming did not end with European arrivals, but entered a new phase.

The journeys made by the Spirit Ancestors are recorded in Dream Tracks. A Dreaming Track can join a number of sites on the landscape, which trace the path of an Ancestral Being. One Dreaming Track shared by many Aboriginal communities is the track of the Spirit Ancestor, the Rainbow Serpent.

The Rainbow Serpent's form is that of a large snake like creature, whose Dreaming Track is always associated with watercourses such as billabongs, rivers, creeks and lagoons. It is the protector of the land, its people and the source of all life. If the Rainbow Serpent is not respected, however, it can also be destructive. Traditionally, if the rules of conduct were broken by plants and animals, the Rainbow Serpent could change them into stones. These stones became hills and mountains. Good plants and animals were rewarded by the serpent and were changed into people. This is how the Aborigines were created.

A powerful symbol of the creative and destructive powers of Nature, the Rainbow Serpent has been a consistent theme in Aboriginal art for over 6,000 years. Some aspect's of the Rainbow Serpent's stories are sacred and can only be told to and by initiated persons.

The Dreaming has different meanings for different Aboriginal people and their stories were once told in over three hundred different languages across the vast continent they belong to. The Dreaming stories are a complex network of knowledge that dominates all the spiritual and physical aspects of Aboriginal life.

The celestial Sky World, where the Old Spirits live, was, and still is, an integral part of Aboriginal culture. Aboriginal people conducted many of their travels at night, over land and sea, and the stars were their guiding lights. Just like every other culture, the Aboriginal clans categorised and named the stars and constellations they could see. Some southern constellations, such as the Seven Sisters or Pleiades, and the Southern Cross, are common amongst Aborignal clans, however, others are as separate as the languages of the people who created them.

Ancient and modern ancestors of the Aboriginal peoples have observed the night sky for more than 40,000 years. Longer than any other living culture. Many of their traditional stories tell of natural events dating thousands of years ago. They applied their knowledge of the stars and constellations for many purposes; for survival; for predicting weather; telling the time; to create a calendar for the changing seasons in order to know the availability of food.

Great and useful stories are, and were, told about the creation of the Earth and the Sky Worlds through the actions of the Spirit Ancestors. According to one legend, the Sun Woman carries a firestick across the sky each day and camps each evening. But in North West Victoria, the Boorong people told how Pupperimbul, the little bird with the red patch above the tail, made the sun. Pupperrimbul made the sun by throwing a prepared Emu egg into space. Before this, the Earth was in darkness. The Pupperrimbul and other creatures are believed to be spiritual representations on Earth of Old Spirits.

Often crossing the hot Australian desert, it makes sense that Aboriginal people travel at night when it is cooler and they can use the stars to guide them. In Summer, in South Australia, the Milky Way is seen travelling from the south to the north, but in Winter, it travels from east to west.

Aboriginal rock engravings have recorded maps of the constellations. One engraving carved by the ancients, in the Gibson Desert, records a Super Nova seen centuries ago, also recorded by the

Chinese.

The Southern Cross was given today's name by Europeans but Aboriginal tribes gave it their own names. To one group, the Lake Tyrell Aborigines, the Southern Cross was a ring-tailed possum, to another group who lived by the sea, it was the stingray, Nunganari, and to another, the Cross is the Emu's footprint.

One group of stars, featured in cosmic mythology throughout the world, The Pleiades, or Seven Sisters, also features widely in Aboriginal stories. Most groups tell how the Seven Sisters ran away from the unwanted approaches of a man, usually Orion, Venus, or the Moon, depending on where the story is told. Other stories depict the sisters as Mallee Fowl eggs in a nest, or tiny fish. Many beautiful stories are told within groups to teach them the positions of the Pleiades and other important stars and planets, and what action that position may deem necessary for the benefit of the family or tribe. The appearance of the Pleiades in the Sky World is linked with the seasonal changes of foods, weather, (frost coming), and ceremonial life.

On Groote Island, the appearance of two stars in Scorpio in the evening sky, towards the end of April, signifies that the wet season has ended and the dry season is about to begin. For over three hundred years, the Macassan fisherman, (from today's Indonesia), traded with the people of northern Australia, the Arnhem, for the sea slug or 'trepang', a delicacy in cooking. Scorpio in the sky indicated the arrival of the fishermen in early December. For the Maori people of New Zealand, Scorpio is the hook which pulled New Zealand out of the sea to become their land.

To the ancient Boorong people, the planet Jupiter is an elder of the Spirit People and husband to the planet Venus, and the Moon represents the quoll or native cat, which has full moon, half moon and crescent moon shapes on its fur. The Milky Way is the smoke of the fires of the Old Spirits. Many aboriginal groups across Australia considered the Sky World to almost mirror the world of the Earth. They could see rivers there, creeks, and hunting grounds, and this is where their spirit or part of it travels after death.

The understanding of astronomy by the indigenous people of Australia is very wide indeed. Much of the detailed knowledge of the stars was and is secret and held only by initiated males. Where those ceremonies ceased, this knowledge has been lost, however ceremonies still continue today in many parts of Australia where this knowledge is passed on to those initiated.

Sadly, the last of the ancient Boorong people died in the nineteenth century. They had lived at Lake Tyrell in Victoria's north west. In the 1840's they shared some of their ancestral stories with a man named William Stanbridge. Mr Stanbridge worked with the elders of the Boorong tribe recording the terms for over thirty stars and constellations alongside its European equivalent. This work has recently been re-discovered. An important work, it will be taught to local Aboriginal children to ensure that this vital knowledge does not disappear like the Boorong people themselves, who have gifted it to their survivors.

New research has revealed that the Boorong people devised their own zodiac, charting the patterns of the seasons and life in old Australia through a unique view of the heavens. The Boorong Zodiac was considered in relation to all aspects of life, just as all zodiacs around the world once were, only this zodiac may even pre-date the Babylonian one by over 23,000 years! In their Sky, the Boorong saw the Gemini twins as a Tortoise and a Fantail Cuckoo. In Capella, they saw a Red Kangaroo, and in Lyra they saw the Mallee Fowl. The disappearance of the Mallee Fowl, indicated the start of that birds laying season on the ground.

In the following pages you will discover your Australian creature star sign. Many creatures are important Totems, (spirits), to Australian Aboriginal and other cultures around the world. These creatures are said to be chosen by the Spirit Ancestors. Totems are sacred and can create a sense of belonging and of spiritual connection to the land and animals, or to others within the Aboriginal clan. Every clan can have a Totem.   Life Totems are believed to accompany people throughout life, whereas Journey Totems reflect a period of time; a time that takes you to a difficult time in life; and will guide you along that path. Journey Totems slip in and out of your life.

A Totem can be a bird, animal, plant or rock and can symbolise the clan's emblem. A Message Totem usually indicates self growth and awakening and will arrive suddenly, randomly or maybe even only once in your life. A Message Totem's appearance brings a unique and powerful message to one whether it appears in a dream or due to an unexpected encounter.

The creatures described in the following pages are listed in the order of the dates of the western star signs for easy reference. If one of the creatures listed is your Totem, disregard the dates and simply look for the name of the creature you are interested in and you will discover a brief description of that creature's significance as a Totem. Enjoy your journey!

Red Kangaroo

Aries

(March 21st – April 20th)

According to some astrologers, those born under this sign of the Australian zodiac are intensely passionate, independent, and self-supporting. However, those traits and the Kangaroo's love of freedom, often disguise the very social side of the Kangaroo. Kangaroo people will support, encourage and foster for the benefit of the wider group. They have a strong nurturing sense and family is very important to them. Sometimes sentimental, people born under this sign can also be a little jealous and possessive.

There are many myths about the Red Kangaroo. One New Guinean myth tells how a kangaroo named Amori followed the first human couple to where they lay down together. After they left, the kangaroo licked up the sperm that was left and became pregnant. The woman and the kangaroo both gave birth to sons. The son of the woman was named Maniwori and the kangaroo's son was called Sisinjori. All things in the cosmos are related according to Aboriginal belief.

According to southern shamanism, the appearance of the Red Kangaroo can signify changes and adventure coming, and to dream of a Kangaroo is symbolic of endurance, strength, mobility and freedom to move.

To some ancient Aborigines, their beloved star, the Sun, was considered a woman, who, when she set, would pass the dwelling places of the dead. At sunrise, the men of the clan would assemble to meet her and invite her to stay with them. To thank the Sun for granting them favours, it was customary for the ancients to leave her a present of a Kangaroo skin, and so, therefore, she appeared each morning to them wearing her red dress.

As a totem animal, some say that the manifestation of the Kangaroo signifies that it is time to break old boundaries and a time to move boldly into new territories and experiences. Because it takes such good care of its young, some southern tribes associate the Red Kangaroo with nurturing and love.

Wombat

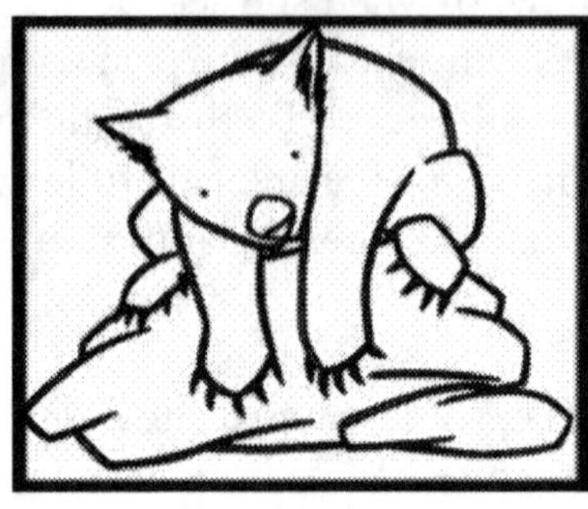

Taurus

(April 21st – May 21st)

According to some Australian astrologers, great strength and endurance are the strongest qualities of those born under the sign of the Wombat. Like the Wombat, people born under this sign have the ability to adapt to their environment and proceed to meet life's challenges with determination. One of Nature's survivors, Wombats are widely respected for their conscientious determination.

One widely known Aboriginal myth tells the story of how Wombats came to have a flat head. Many, many years ago, when Kangaroo and Wombat were still men, they were very friendly. They hunted and lived together and shared the same camping ground. Wombat had a comfortable home made of bark and soft leaves, but Kangaroo loved to sleep beside a bright beautiful fire beneath the sky world of the Spirit Ancestors.

One night, during the rainy season, a great storm arose. The wind wailed eerily and the rain was so torrential that the stars could not be seen. Kangaroo's fire was quickly extinguished that night and he began to chill so he decided to ask his good friend Wombat to shelter him for the night. Wombat implicated that there wasn't enough room for them both by rejecting Kangaroo's suggestions for any space to lie down in, in his home, even a tiny corner. Miserable, Kangaroo went back outside and sat beside the damp embers of his campfire.

The storm became even worse after a time, so Kangaroo asked
Wombat again for shelter. Again, his request was refused. So angered
was Kangaroo, by his friends selfish responses, he picked up a rock and
struck Wombat on the head with it, shouting, that from that day forth
Wombat and all his descendants would have flat heads and live in dark
holes in the ground.

Wombat was so furious after this outburst that he threw a spear at
Kangaroo as he walked away. As the spear lodged itself into the lower
part of Kangaroo's spine, Wombat shouted that all of Kangaroo's
descendants would from that day forth have to use a tail to run with and
would never have a home of their own to shelter in. Since that day, both
Kangaroo and Wombat have become animals and Wombats have flat
heads, live in the ground, and Kangaroos have long tails and no particular
home!

As a totem animal, it is said that the manifestation of the Wombat
signifies strong psychic skills and those with this totem often find
themselves in situations where their psychic skills are tested, criticised,
ignored or praised. They must honour their truth and not be intimidated
by others.

Pygmy Sugar Glider

Gemini

(May 22nd – June 21st)

Those born under the sign of the Pigmy Sugar Glider are said to be quick, agile and intelligent, with a natural ability for handling pressure. Pygmy Sugar Gliders have dual natures, one of the air and trees, and one of earth. Associated with graceful movements and charm, Pygmy Sugar Glider people will glide from one project to another in order to nurture their very active minds.

The Pygmy Sugar Glider is a possum, native to eastern and northern Australia, New Guinea, and the Bismarck Archipelago. A tiny marsupial, this inquisitive little glider is, according to Aboriginal belief, one of the sacred animals of the Moon.

Many Aboriginal myths speak of the Moon as a male, and to those people, the Moon was husband to all women. Young girls were once warned not to look too closely at the Moon Man, in case they would fall pregnant. A symbol of fertility and hope, Aboriginal clans believed too, that the Moon also conferred this power to reproduce on plants and animals as well as women.

One tradition tells how the Moon Cycle works through the story of how once, when the Moon Man lived with his sister, the Dugong, she would collect lily bulbs and lotus roots for them to eat. During these gatherings, to her dismay, she was constantly bitten by leeches, and one day, she declared that she was giving up land life and going to live in the sea. The Moon asked his sister what he should do, and she told him he could stay in the sky, but first he would have to die.

The Moon considered this, and decided that he would die, but would always return to life again. His sister the Dugong, declared that was up to him but when she died she wouldn't return so he would have to pick up her bones. To this, the Moon replied that he would grow himself thin enough to follow her down into the sea, that he would leave his bones there, become a pure spirit, and then after three days, he would return to the sky. Traditional belief states that the nautilus shells are the bones of dead Moons.

The Pygmy Sugar Glider is not the only animal sacred to the Moon. Emu, Crab and Frog join him. Bone and Boomerang are also related to it. The master of death and rebirth, the Moon brings a promise of survival and as a totem animal of the Moon, the nocturnal little Pygmy Sugar Glider symbolises liveliness, survival, and adaptability.

Koala

Cancer

(June 22nd – July 22nd)

Those born under the sign of Koala are believed by some Australian astrologers to be the guardians of the World. Warm and cherishing, Koala's have strong family ties, and are associated with strength amongst adversity. Koala's love life and are loving and supportive members of any group. No burden is too heavy to bear for the Koala personality.

Ancient mythology records that cute and gentle Koala once befriended the amphibious monster that inhabits inland waterways in Australia, Bunyip. This friendship was considered by all the other native bears to be a dangerous one and they feared it would bring about the destruction of their species. The Koala concerned, would, night after night, go down to the swamp to drink, and spend long periods of time there in conversation with Bunyip before returning to its mountain tree top home.

News reached the other bears that the unhealthy friendship was so strong that the Koala was leaving its baby alone in the trees all night and they became very concerned. The Koala's knew that Man hated and feared Bunyip too and did something to protect themselves against the monster. One night, the native bears decided to watch a ceremony attended by Man to discover exactly how he protected himself from Bunyip. Before the men arrived at the ceremonial spot, the bears took up positions in the trees and almost closed their eyes so that the light from Man's fire would not reflect in their eyes and reveal their presence.

As the bears watched from the branches, the Men came and set up camp, and once the fire was lit, they sat in a circle around it. Soon, a Medicine Man joined them, who was painted in stripes of yellow and white clay to which tufts of white cotton were clinging. He danced round the fire shaking his spear and sang in a language the bears could not understand. In the morning, after the men departed, the bears decided that the painted markings on the Medicine Man must hold the magic that reached the Spirit of Man and came to protect them, so one of the bears asked to be painted in the same way.

Before dusk that day, the painted bear went up the mountain to where the Koala who had befriended the Bunyip lived. He found the Koala's baby alone so Painted Bear picked it up, held it, and whispered to the baby that when its mother returned it must cling tightly to her back and never let go, and he put some paint on the baby too.

The magic markings were effective and the baby clung tightly to hits mother and did not let go of her no matter how hard she tried to dislodge it. Painted Bear visited the mountain Koala mother, and told her that no bears must associate with the dangerous Bunyip, so, for the benefit of all, the marks that had been painted on his fur, would now forever appear on the fur on the heads of all Koalas to remind and protect them. From then on, they would get all the water they needed from the Eucalyptus trees. Ever since that time, so has it been.

A gentle, if lethargic creature, this animal totem may indicate a time of calmness, peace and love.

Frilled Neck Lizard

Leo

(23rd July – August 22nd)

The most dramatic and colourful of all of the Australian lizards, it is said that those people born under the sign of the Frilled Neck Lizard are incredibly flamboyant and attract a lot of attention. A brave heart, although instinct may tell the Frilled Neck Lizard to run from danger, if it cannot, it will face up to its enemies with heroic determination. Protective by nature, Frilled Neck Lizard people are associated with loyalty.

Aboriginal myth states that the Frilled Neck Lizard was originally a man who was smooth and sleek. Once, a long time ago, during a ceremony, his mind wandered and he sang the wrong song. He was punished by the elders who turned him into a lizard as a warning to people who will not submit to tribal discipline.

In Australian mythology, the sky gods made animals, birds and plants, which they then formed into human beings. Each individual belongs to the totem that is that plant, bird or animal from which he was transformed. Often, stories of the experiences of the descendants of these Spirit Ancestors tell how the landscape was formed.

One such legend tells the story of an old man, a Frilled Neck Lizard who made a beaked boomerang which, at first, he threw to the east. When it returned, he then threw it to the west and with these two throws he carved out the course of the Roper River. The man had two sons with him who were amazed to see that a great rain cloud appeared that filled the carved river course with water. However, at the same time a stormy wind appeared and all three of them were blown into the water. The old man and his younger son were drowned, but the eldest son managed to reach the riverbank. Such was his sorrow, that he made long corrobborees on the bank, singing to the Spirit Ancestors in his grief. The old man, who had sunk to the bottom of the river, was turned into a rock, as was his spirit child with him.

After a while, exhausted, the eldest son lay down on the bank and his parts were turned into stone. The site by the Roper River became a traditional site for Frilled Lizard men to make their ceremonies.

The lizard as a totem symbolises the dream world beyond time and space and its teaching holds one responsible for every single event in ones life, consciously or not, because everything springs from ones wishes and fears.

Echidna

Virgo

(23rd August – September 22nd)

Those born under the sign of Echidna are said to possess a highly developed sense of self-preservation and will make great efforts to find an environment that accommodates their contentment. The Echidna has a clear, alert, and analytical mind and is very protective of itself. The cool exterior of the quill covered Echidna can only be penetrated by those that it finds acceptable. Only to them will Echidna people reveal themselves or their vulnerability, and if confronted, the Echidna will disappear from sight.

Amongst the ancient Aborignals, there is a tradition that Echidna was once a woman. She was friendly with a long necked man and they went hunting together. One day, they both saw a snail, and began quarrelling as to who should get to eat the delicacy. The quarrel turned into a fight and, in a rage, the man threw spears all over the woman. She managed to reach a flat-bottomed rock and threw it at the man. The rock knocked him down and stuck to him. He became the long necked turtle, she the Echidna, covered in spines.

There are many widely known myths about the short beaked Echidna in the animistic culture of the indigenous people of Australia that relate similarly to how this totem animal got its spines. Another example explains that Echidna was created when a group of hungry young men went hunting one night and stumbled across a Wombat.

110

They threw spears at the Wombat, but lost sight of it in the darkness. The Wombat adapted the spears as its own defence and turned into an Echidna.

The Echidna was a totem for many groups including the Noongar people from western Australia who called it Nyingarn.

The totem Echidna teaches us of openness and to retain a child-like sense of wonder and trust in a divine plan where everything will turn out all right. Friendliness and openness can unlock the hearts of others and Echidna symbolises sharing for and of love and joy.

Galah

Libra

(September 23rd – October 22nd)

According to some Australian astrologers, those born under the sign of the Galah seek harmony and balance in life. Socially aware, Galahs enjoy group activities and love to brighten up the dullest places. Galah people avoid messy problems, will warn other creatures of danger, and display a strong sense of allegiance to others. Its happy nature combined with confidence makes the Galah a very balanced creation.

The Galah is a member of the Cockatoo family and there have been many dreamtime stories told about them. One story tells how, ages ago, in the dreamtime, when many of the beautiful birds and animals in the bush were men, men did not know the secret of obtaining fire.

One morning, an old man awoke before the sun had climbed the mountains and he saw fire gleaming through the trees of the forest. He crept nearer to see what was happening and he saw Mar, the red crested Cockatoo, take fire from under his crest and light his way through the trees with it. The old man followed the Cockatoo quickly but in his hurry he trod on a dry stick and Mar the Cockatoo turned and saw him. Mar threw a spear at the old man, who fled.

The old man travelled far and just when he was suffering from exhaustion and thirst, he met a tribe who helped him. He told them the Cockatoos fire secret and the tribe became very excited and decided to invite Mar the Cockatoo to a great corroboree where they would steal the fire from him.

Mar accepted their invitation and whilst the singing and dancing was going on he was offered a choice piece of Kangaroo meat to eat. He refused this, but when he was offered the skin of the Kangaroo, he accepted that and immediately took it away to his camp, so when the feats was over the tribe still did not have the fire. However, one of the members of the tribe had followed Mar to find out where the Cockatoo's camp was and he too saw Mar take the fire from his crest feathers, thus the old man's story was confirmed. The tribe decided then, that Tatkanna the Robin should journey to Mar's camp and take the fire.

Tatkanna set off early the next morning and he arrived at the Cockatoo's camp just in time to see Mar take some fire from his crest, light a fire stick and singe the hair off the Kangaroo skin he'd been gifted. Tatkanna the Robin was so eager to steal the fire that he got too close to it and singed his breast feathers. Mar spotted Tatkanna but the brave little Robin seized a fire stick and made off as quickly as he could. On the way, Tatkanna set fire to some dry grass and soon the bush was ablaze, roaring like the sound of floodwaters!

Birds and animals had to flee to find shelter. When Mar the Cockatoo discovered that the fire was stolen from him and beyond his control, he was very angry and went off in search of Tatkanna the Robin to kill him. Tatkanna was petrified when Mar finally arrived at the tribe's campsite looking for him but, to help him, his friend Quartung the Kookaburra took up the quarrel on his behalf. Quartung was so badly beaten in the fight with Mar, he flew to the trees where Kookaburras have remained ever since. Mar, the red crested Cockatoo returned to his camp in disdain having lost his fire. He still has a beautiful red crest and is known now as Leadbeater's Cockatoo. Tarkanna the Robin became known as Robin Redbreast, and the tribe of men kept their fire.

If you look closely under the Galah Cockatoo's crest, you will discover something you won't find on the red crested bird, a bald patch. According to myth, this bald patch is due to an accident that an ancient Galah once had whilst watching a plain brown lizard throwing the especially curved boomerangs that return to the thrower. Whilst showing off, Lizard threw one that hit Galah on the head. Galah seized Lizard with her beak and rolled with him in the bush so much so that her blood smeared over the lizard. Ever since that time there have been lizards in the lands of the Galah that are coloured reddish brown and are covered with spikes just like the prickles of the bindeah bush.

Perhaps this story is the reason that the Galah Cockatoo is flushed pink, adding beauty to the amazing happy hearted family of the Cockatoo!

Red Back Spider

Scorpio

(October 23rd – November 21st)

Those born under this sign are said to have alluring personalities and intense desires, two traits that capture the attention of others. Disliking new situations, the Red Back Spider will go it alone to continue to improve the quality of an existing project, (where others might have given up), until it gets it right. Although the Red Back Spider is solitary by nature, once it makes a commitment it will never give up. The Red Back Spider is associated with intense experiences.

Spiders play a significant role in the lives and beliefs of many cultures in the world including Australia and the islands surrounding it. In the Banks Islands, of the coast of Australia, spider motifs appear in bark paintings and tattoos. In the southern Malakula island, spider web cloth is used as a base for sacred artworks and also for making coverings for the head and body required for male rituals. Certain Spider Spirit Ancestors are believed to play a part in the early stages of life after death.

To make the web cloth, spider webs are collected on a bamboo pole which has been splayed open at one end. People walk through the bush in the morning pulling down the webs with this pole. The webs accumulate on the pole until a thick matted cloth is formed. This cloth is supple, but tough and hardwearing, and fairly waterproof and resistant to rot.

In the Northern Territories too, Aboriginal people have depicted spiders in their bark and rock paintings. For the Rembarrnga/Kyne people in central Arnhem Land, Australia, spiders are an important Barnungku clan totem. Spiders in their webs are associated with a sacred rock on the clan estate and the design is connected with major regional ceremony. These spider totems provide a link with neighbouring clans who also use spider totems in their rituals.

Further away in the Pacific Ocean, a wonderful creation story relating to Spider comes to us from the little island called Nauru. The story tells how, in the beginning there was only a saltless sea and an Ancient Spider who floated above in endless space.

One day, Ancient Spider took up a tridacna mussel from the sea, and after studying its roundness, and studying its shape, he wondered if he could find away to open it a little so that he might go inside it. Eventually, for the shell was extremely strong, he succeeded in opening the great shell just enough to crawl inside it. Because the Sun and Moon had not been made yet, Ancient Spider could see nothing, and since the shell was quite small inside, he could not stand upright. Exploring by touch, he discovered a snail. Ancient Spider put the snail under his arm and lay down and slept for three days directing some of his ancient power to the snail. When the three days were over, he lay the snail aside and explored the space within the shell further. This time he found another, larger snail. Ancient Spider did the same with that one and after the three days sleep, Ancient Spider asked the smallest of the snails if he could lift the shell roof a little so that they might all sit up.

The little snail raised the shell slightly, and for this great deed, Ancient Spider made him into the Moon and set him west of the upper part of the shell. By the light now shining from Moon, Ancient Spider saw a large worm or grub in the shell, who, when asked if he could, raised the roof of the shell even higher. As the worm pushed with all his might, salty sweat ran down his body and collected in the lower part of the shell and spilled over. It became the living salty sea.

The upper part of the shell was raised as high as it could be risen and became the sky, but the poor worm died. Ancient Spider, from the other, larger snail, made the Sun and set it on the east side of the lower part of the shell. Then, the lower part of the shell became the Earth. Ancient Spider is also known as Areop-Enap.

    As a totem the spider is the totem of responsibility and infinity. Its body and legs both show the number eight representing infinity. According to mythology, the spider embodies the unlimited number of possibilities within creation. The totem spider instructs us to accept responsibility for anything that happens in our lives and therefore that we weave the web of our destiny. The victim who becomes caught in the web has not yet understood that lesson and is entangled in a reality that appears unchangeable.

Kookaburra

Sagittarius

(November 22nd – December 20th)

Those born under this sign are said to be guided by the planet Jupiter, and may possess inexhaustible energy, according to some Australian astrologers. Kookaburra people approach life with a passion. Involved in a search for self-fulfilment the Kookaburra directs its concerns towards large issues on which it will focus its mental energy in a smiling, enlightened manner. Associated with truth and justice, the Kookaburra awakens others to self-awareness and social consciousness.

According to Aboriginal mythology, people in ancient days had an affinity with such birds as parrots, cockatoos, and other birds, but the Kookaburra was not included until one day, a man who had an affinity with a lyrebird arranged a competition. He proclaimed that his lyrebird could imitate and improve the song of any bird. People who belonged to parrots, wattles and other birds, brought their birds along to the competition and, sure enough, the lyrebird not only imitated them but also excelled each in their song.

One bird sat on a limb that day, watching and listening to the proceedings, then, just before dark, made its own efforts. The lyrebird imitated it perfectly. But the other bird was not finished and called out again in another key. Again the lyrebird imitated it perfectly, but the bird changed its song again and again until the lyrebird became confused. It could not continue to imitate the Kookaburra who laughed at its mocking of all other birds and it was this laugh that the lyrebird could not properly mock. Ever since that time, Kookaburra people have been regarded as people of great importance.

In Aboriginal dreamtime mythology, the Kookaburra's laughing call was said to awaken even the Sky People, and so, on the day that the Sun was made, the Sky deity ordered the Kookaburra to laugh every dawn to wake up the world as soon as the morning star paled.

As a totem, Kookaburra also symbolises the awakening of the fires of passion to fuel inspiration and its message tells us to laugh in the face of adversity no matter how many times others may mock our efforts.

Goanna

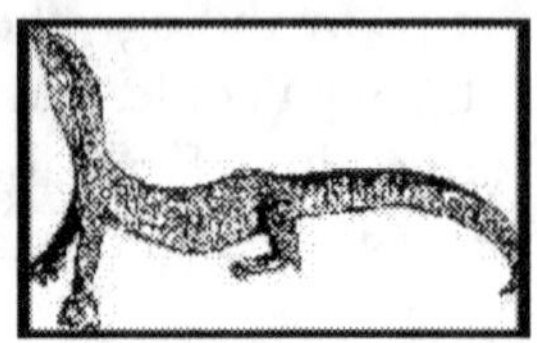

Capricorn

(December 21st – January 19th)

Like the Goanna, people born under this sign are said to be sensible, determined, clever and superior. They may appear to be icy cool, even uncaring, but that is only shyness and Goanna people adopt a serious approach towards love, according to some Australian astrologers.

Long, long ago, in the dreamtime, in the days when animals walked on two legs and were like men, two very different tribes lived together. They were the Goanna people and the Porcupine people. The tribes' ancestors had come from different directions originally and so they had an uneasy association. The Porcupines were good hunters and mocked the Goannas who were not. The Goannas tended to take to the trees and live on the sugar bags of the native bees. The Goannas were, however, clever, and good thieves, and would often steal from the stores of the Porcupines.

One day, the Goannas declared that they were that day going to bring more food home than the Porcupines. The Porcupines laughed and hunted harder than ever, certain that they could prove beyond a shadow of a doubt that they were the best hunting tribe. The Goannas did nothing but sleep all that day in the hot sun. When the exhausted Porcupines returned to the camp, the Goannas told them that they had found even the sugarbags of the bees scarce, but to make up for their lack of bounty, they volunteered to cook for both tribes and encouraged the Porcupine tribal members to sleep by the fire whilst they prepared and cooked the food. The tired hunters gladly accepted this suggestion.

The Goannas roasted the food alright, but each roasted piece was passed from one Goanna member to another until all the cooked food was hidden in the trees. Occasionally, a sleepy Porcupine would awaken briefly to the delicious smell of the cooking, only to be told to go back to sleep until the food was ready.

When the last piece of meat was ready, a Goanna tried to remove it from the fire and knocked over a burning log. The log rolled towards a sleeping Porcupine and scorched him awake. His screams woke up the others and they realised what was going on. One of the Porcupines grabbed a burning stick from the fire and hit out at as many fleeing Goannas as he could, leaving black stripes all over the Goannas' golden bodies. From that day, the tribes parted company and to this day Goannas still have the distinctive yellow and black stripes.

The lizard symbolises the dream world beyond time and space and, according to Aboriginal mythology, it can see into the future and knows how to use dreams to create a future reality. The Goanna, it is said, uses these talents in order to calculate a favourable outcome for itself.

Emu

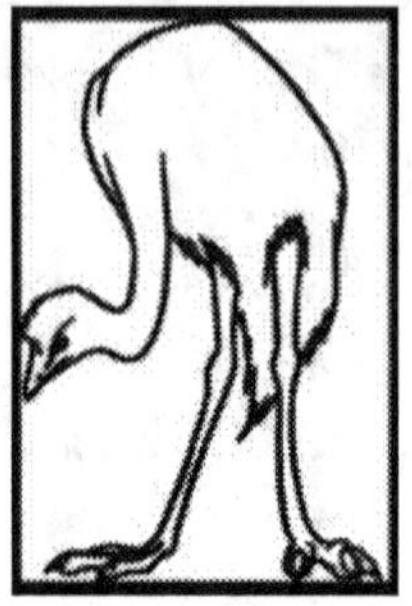

Aquarius

(January 20th – February 19th)

According to some Australian astrologers, those born under the sign of Emu are excellent communicators, inquisitive, and great visionaries. Individuals born under this sign are not afraid to voice their opinions especially when it is about something they passionately believe in. Emu's are extremely observant and are associated with clear perspective.

For thousands of years, Emu has been regarded by Aboriginals as an important object in the night sky. To some Aboriginal Elders, Emu is the dark shadow called the Coal Sack that sits next to the Southern Cross. Its neck passes across through the Pointer stars and its body lies across the constellation Scorpio. The orientation of the Emu shadow in the sky at certain times of the year indicates to Aboriginal Elders when certain ceremonies should take place. This shadow is the blackness between the stars and the bands of the Milky Way, and is most easily seen from May to September.

Aboriginal mythology speaks of a time when Emu once had very long wings and made her home in the sky. One day, she looked through the clouds down to Earth and she saw a variety of birds gathering near a lagoon. Some of the birds were singing, others dancing, and the Kookaburras were chuckling to themselves. The Emu felt like dancing herself and, inspired by this joyful sight, she flew down from the sky to the lagoon. The native birds were surprised when they saw her and were jealous of her long beautiful wings. When she asked them if they would teach her to dance, they told her she would need shorter wings like them first, so she allowed them to clip her wings.

Later, when the other birds all flew away, Emu realised that she could no longer fly and could not go home. In time, she made Earth her home and although she could never fly again, her legs became stronger and she could dance and run very well. She laid huge clutches of eggs and her family spread throughout the land. A member of her own family once quarrelled with her and, after trampling on all of her eggs, lifted the last one and threw it up into the sky. Emu prayed it would be safe as she watched it travel higher and higher towards the clouds. The egg struck a pile of firewood that had been gathered by a Cloud Man. The wood burst into flames and flooded the Earth with light. The light prompted the plants and trees to produce flowers and fruits never seen before. Birds gathered and sang praises to the sky in thanks for the warmth they felt. When the fire went out, the Cloud Man decided he would gather wood every night from the sky forests in order to light up the Earth every day. Thus Emu's egg became the Sun, whom all birds welcome at dawn, and praise in the evening.

As a totem, Emu is a symbol of blame and forgiveness. Often depicted as a creature who is troublesome and misses opportunities in dreamtime stories, the message from Emu tells us to examine our own desires and fears, in order to recognise unrealistic expectations, and to understand that harmony can come from simple ambitions.

Platypus

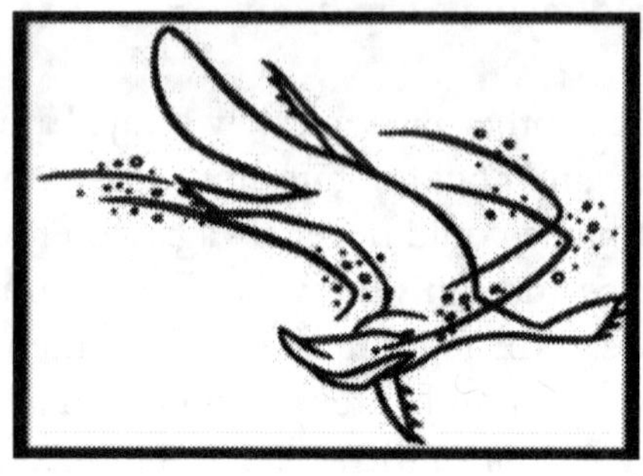

Pisces

(February 20th – March 20th)

The Platypus is rarely seen and, according to some Australian astrologers, those born under this sign can be timid, demure and sensitive. Platypus people often lose themselves in their dream world and are happiest employed in environments that suit their sensitivity. Platypus is associated with the arts and with the right encouragement those born under this sign can be very successful in this field.

Probably the planet Earth's most unusual looking creature, there are quite a few mythological stories that relate to the origins of this extraordinary, egg laying, amphibious mammal. One dreamtime story tells how one of the Spirit Ancestors, a woman, came down to Earth from the sky to awaken new life forms. Where she walked, ice melted and formed the rivers, streams and seas. When she trod on land, plants, mosses, trees and grass, appeared, and then, with her breath, she blew life into air and created winds.

Once the planet was fully prepared, she awoke the spirits of all the birds, animals and insects. This done, she instructed them to enjoy their lives where everything was provided for them, then she returned to the sky.

At first, all was well and everyone got along with everyone else, but then envy crept in and some creatures disrupted the peace of others. The

Spirit Ancestor returned and gave them all the power of transformation so that they could change themselves into whatever form they wished in order to content them. Once again she returned to her home in the sky only this time saying she would be back to see how they all were.

When she returned, she was not pleased with their transformations. The rats had transformed themselves into new creatures called bats. There were giant fish and lizards with blue tongues and feet. But one creature had so transformed itself, even she couldn't remember its original form! It was a furry animal with a bill like a duck, only it had teeth too. It had the tail of a beaver, and even more extraordinary, it laid eggs even though it was a mammal! This was Platypus, of course.

Spirit Ancestor removed the power of transformation from the creatures and gave birth to two children. One was the Morning Star and the other was Moon. They too had children, who were sent to Earth. It was they who became our ancestors according to Aboriginal mythology.

As a totem, the Platypus represents female energy. People with that energy practice free love without power. The message Platypus sends is that there is a power in sharing and kindness; that if we follow the flow of the stream of life and practice unconditional love, we will discover that everything we need, we will receive.

The Author

Marilyn Reid, lives in the Highlands of Scotland. 'MYTHICAL STAR SIGNS' is Marilyn's second book. This follows her very successful first book 'MYTHICAL FLOWER STORIES'.

She is also a commissioned playwright trained in Theatre Arts. Marilyn has been involved in the past in the tutoring, directing, writing for and setting up of many Community Arts Projects.
Her main interests are World Cultures, History, Folklore and Mythology . Marilyn's plays have been performed on the stages of Scotland on local radio, and in schools, many of which were written she wrote her previous name 'Cameron.'   Her most recent play, 'Silver Tides' is currently in rehearsals for participation in the Highland 2007 festival.

In recent years, Marilyn has concentrated on writing books and content for the internet too. Some of her prior publications are currently on sale as information booklets 'The Broch Builders' (2002) and 'Glenelg Shadows' (2003), 'The Prevailing Legends of Nessie and her World Wide Cousins' (2005), 'Go Wild in Scotland' (2005), to name but a few of her projects.

Marilyn is currently working on a new publication of her plays, on two new books, and in schools and communities running Writer's Workshops.